Never Really a Child

By
Judy Lambert

PublishAmerica
Baltimore

First printing

At the specific preference of the author, PublishAmerica allowed this work to remain exactly as the author intended, verbatim, without editorial input.

ISBN: 1-4241-4201-6
PUBLISHED BY PUBLISHAMERICA, LLLP
www.publishamerica.com
Baltimore

Printed in the United States of America

This book is dedicated to Brian and Nancy, David and Missy, with the hope that reading this, they will understand why family is so important and how special they and their families are to Dad and I.

Also, to our grandchildren that they may know their grandfather's story and appreciate the lessons to be learned from it. Regardless of what life gives you, with faith in God and a positive attitude, you can be whatever you chose to be.

I would like to give special thanks to my grandson Joshua, without whose questions and insistence in knowing grandpa's story, this would have not been completed. Thanks, Josh, for the push I needed.

I would like to thank Paul's brother, Lee, and sister, Franie, for all the hours they spent recalling their childhood along with Paul. They gave me valuable information and insight into what their life was like at that time. Franie, being the oldest gave me a great deal of information about their Dad's tragic end, which Paul was too young to remember. I appreciate the honesty and openness of both of them.

I would like to thank Mountain Mission School for the care and teaching they gave Paul. I hate to think what his life may have been like had it not been for them being there to rescue him. I am glad to report that they continue to this day, providing care and teaching to countless children in the same spirit as when Pop Hurley was alive. Thank you seems so inadequate.

Last, but certainly not least, I would like to thank my husband, Paul, whose story this is, for the hours he spent recalling his childhood. For being willing to expose himself and his fears, for sharing personal feelings and some unpleasant memories, and for insisting that the good memories be recorded, also.

S tanding shyly in the bedroom doorway of our three-room house, I was secretly hoping Dad would notice me. He was sitting on a straight-back chair, turned backwards, tilted forward on two legs, as he always did, watching Mom cook his breakfast. I was startled when I heard him say, "What you doin' up, boy?"

"I just wanted to see you, Dad," I replied quietly.

"Well, git on over here," he said motioning to his lap. It was so rare, with eight of us at home, to get any time alone with Dad. When he beckoned, I eagerly ran and jumped into his lap. This was such a treat as Dad was usually gone to the coalmine by the time any of us were out of bed. The strong smell of his coffee filled my nose, as he absentmindedly petted me while waiting for his breakfast. Knowing that Dad never took time to eat at the mine, Mom always tried to feed him a good breakfast before he left for work. Biscuits, eggs, fried potatoes and some fried fish would hold him until supper. Then, just as quickly as the moment had begun for me, it ended. Breakfast was ready and he set me down on the floor. Meals were not social occasions in our house, just a necessary part of survival. Dad finished eating, grabbed his round, tin water pail and took off for the mine. I stood in the doorway watching him go. As he got to the creek that ran in front of the house, he stopped, turned around and dashed back to the house. "I forgot my hat, "he yelled at Mom before she could ask. Mom got a strange, unsettled look on her face as he grabbed his hat off the peg and was gone.

Asking her what was wrong, she simply stated, "Once you leave the house, you never come back for anything. Just brings bad luck." Being only three and a half years old, that meant nothing to me. I sensed that Mom was bothered, but I had no idea how true her words would prove to be.

The house began to stir as my sisters woke up to help Mom get breakfast for the rest of us. Being the oldest girl, Franie, was expected to be our "second Mom." She grumbled about all the babies, so much to do and how she had to take care of us before she could go to school.

"I'm never having any kids," she wailed as she turned Walt, Lee and I over to Madeline to dress. Madeline was the "protector" of us boys and always stepped in when Franie or Mom had lost patience with us. Johnny and Doug, being older, had dressed, finished their chores, and sat down at the table as Loretta helped Mom finish cooking. Finally, everyone was fed and the older ones had left for school. Franie had to stay home again as Mom had come down with another one of her sick headaches. She had them a lot it seemed. Life was hard in the coal camps and unfortunately for Franie, that meant she had to take over the burden of the house and kids when Mom wasn't able to function.

Dad and Mom had moved to southern West Virginia from Ohio in 1921 to be near Mom's family. She had never liked Ohio and wanted to be near her Dad and sisters. Dad had worked in an iron foundry in Ohio, so he reasoned coal mining couldn't be any worse and he would have done anything to please Mom. A strong, handsome man with a square jaw, twinkling blue eyes and a shock of brown hair, he sure wasn't afraid of hard work.

With a wife, a son and three daughters, he needed a job quickly and the coalmines always needed men. He worked daylight to dark without a complaint. Men did what it took to survive and support their families. Dad was no different.

Harold, Dad, Mom holding Loretta with Madeline and Franie in front

Mining was a dangerous job. There was almost no government regulation for mine owners to worry about and, unfortunately, the health and safety of the miners was oft times their last concern. The owners built coal camps of rows of small, wooden houses, mostly the same. There was no thought of attractiveness or quality, simply something thrown together for the least amount of money to house as many miners and their families as possible. Painted white originally, most were now a dusty, gray from the coal dust settling on them. Most of the camps had some type of one or two room school for the children and almost all of them had a church. The mine owners paid the teachers and preachers, thus adding to their profit by obligating them to the mines, also. The miners were paid in scrip, which was a type of money that bore the inscription of the mine company. It was only accepted at the company store and every camp had one. You could get about anything you needed at them, but the prices were usually inflated to make more profit and keep the miners in debt to the mine owners. With all of this, the mines produced a healthy profit for the owners and coal mining flourished in West Virginia.

The family consisted of a son, Harold, and three daughters, Frances, Madeline and Loretta. Between 1922 and 1928, it expanded to include four more sons, John, Doug, Walter and Paul. While Harold and the girls had all been born in Ohio, the boys were all born after they had moved to West Virginia. Although a typical size family for the time, it was difficult for Dad to provide much more than the basics needed for survival.

Typhoid fever was always a fear in the coal camps, with the water supply often contaminated by the mines. Christmas of 1929 was especially hard as the fever was running rampant in our camp. Harold was fourteen years old when he was stricken and Loretta and Madeline soon took ill, also. Everyone worked tirelessly to save them, but on Dec. 27, the good Lord took Harold. What a blow! It was a tough time for Dad and Mom, losing their first-born child. Struggling to see the girls through the fever, they barely had time to grieve for him. Thankfully, the girls survived. I don't know if parents ever get over losing a child and everyone they knew that bitter winter of 1929 had lost someone it seemed. Somehow, life goes on. The remainder of the family has to be fed, housed, and clothed. Dad and Mom coped as best they could and slowly life returned to some degree of normalcy.

By the fall of 1930, Mom was with child again. Franie was annoyed, that even though she was almost fourteen, she was told nothing about Mom's condition. At the time, childbearing simply happened, with no explanation to anyone, including daughters, about the how or why. Childbirth usually occurred at home and, if you were fortunate, a midwife was present to help you. And so it was, that on April 11, 1931, Mom gave birth to another boy. Lee had the same sandy, red hair and fair skin as his oldest sister and she took him to heart immediately, in spite of herself.

Dad wasn't one to show much affection toward us when we were no longer babies, according to my sisters. Babies were allowed to be cuddled, but after that, it was his role to teach us responsibility, respect, and discipline. It was Mother's role to care for our other needs. He taught the older ones the things he felt was important. He took us to church every Sunday, even when Mom was too sick to go with us. He taught us to care for one another and to always be there for each other. To be honest and remember that a person was only as good as their word. Take care of yourself and work hard for what you want because no one owes you anything if you're too lazy to work. Later on, my sisters would make sure I knew everything that Dad had stood for and believed. He took us up on the mountain for picnics in good weather and taught us how to gather and shell hickory nuts and walnuts. He showed us where to find the bluest, sweetest huckleberries and to run if you smelled cucumbers near them. That was a sign that a copperhead snake was in the berries. Even though I was young, he showed me where and how to gather greens for Mom.

She was a pretty woman, but not as strong emotionally as some other women seemed to be. With only a third grade education, she depended on Dad for everything. After they were married, he had taught her to read and write. At least enough to do basic things she needed to do. Coming from a family of seven girls, her father didn't believe book learning was necessary for girls. He had refused to call any of them by name, but referred to them all as son, disappointed he had only girls. Regardless, Mom worshipped her Father, as she did Dad, and whatever they said was gospel to her. She never questioned any decision they made about anything.

After moving around a few times, we had settled in Stirrett, West Virginia, in the southwestern portion of the state. After crossing the footbridge a few steps from our house, Dad only had a short walk down the road a piece to the mine. It was a beautiful fall morning and Dad was whistling to himself, as he went along. October skies are clear and the air is as good as it ever gets in the coal camps. Life didn't feel near as dreary on days like this.

*Early fall, 1932 Loretta, Madeline, Franie, Lee
Walt, Johnny, Paul, Doug*

The shrill pitch of the coalmine whistle broke the quiet of that sunny, October 4 day in 1932. Everyone knew the signal and what it meant. There had been an accident at the mine! Every able-bodied man rushed to the spot of the accident. This was not the first time for most of them; accidents were an unfortunate part of life in the coalmines. Arriving at the opening, as the survivors emerged, the rescuers were told that a pillar had dislodged and a portion of the roof of the mine had collapsed. Knowing that every second counts in a collapse, they wasted no time rushing inside to look for more survivors. Quickly, they located someone face down in the dirt. The pillar that was supporting the roof had dislodged and swinging free, hit the man in the back of the head. Turning him over, they were shocked to realize "Steam Shovel" had been killed. They had nicknamed Dad "Steam Shovel" because he worked so hard and fast the men thought he looked like a machine. Hurrying to remove him for fear the roof might still collapse on them, they were devastated. Relieved that no one else had been killed, they did not want to believe that this could have happened to "Steam Shovel." Stunned and distressed, they knew they had to deliver the news to Mom in person.

"We can't let her hear this from just anyone, " Sam, the foreman commented to the two men who had pulled his body out. "Steam Shovel had a passel of kids, too. This is going to be hard on all of them. " Knowing it was the right thing to do, they began the short walk to her house to deliver their sad news.

Franie, 15 years old, stood over the ironing board, frozen in place by the whistle blowing. She had always feared that sound, knowing that any accident at the mine would likely be bad news for someone.

A young boy came running and jumped onto the porch yelling, "It's your Dad. He's been killed." Bad news rarely came softly in our part of the country. Refusing to believe him, Franie ran him off the porch. Mom had stopped hanging the wash on the line when she heard the yelling. Stepping out from the back of the house, just in time to see the boy run off, she had no idea what news he had brought. However, as soon as she saw the men from the mine crossing the footbridge leading to our house she instinctively knew it was bad news. Turning away, as Sam reached out to console her, she collapsed. It would be weeks before she could absorb the news.

Johnny and Doug came dashing in from school when word reached them. That kind of news spreads like wildfire in a coal camp. Madeline and Loretta were a little slower; not wanting to believe what they knew to be true. Loretta had been Dad's "little princess" and she was inconsolable when faced with the truth.

"It just can't be," she wailed to Mom. "Not my Daddy. " Unable to comprehend or comfort anyone, Mom just walked away, leaving her to cry alone. Franie recalled going to church with Dad the night before because Mom wasn't up to it and he really wanted someone to go with him.

"He wore his blue, serge suit," she recalled, "and he and I sang a special. It was "God Be With You Till We Meet Again." Maybe he knew something was going to happen to him," she mused to no one in particular. Madeline had simply set about taking care of the little boys, trying to keep them from being upset about something they did not understand and keeping her own grief to herself. Johnny and Doug, as boys are prone to do, went off by themselves to try to come to grips with their hurt and despair. They knew they would be expected to be strong for their Mom and sisters, even though they were young and had no one to console them.

The next few days passed in a blur of family, friends and

tears. My sisters scrubbed and dressed Walt, Lee and I for the funeral. Walt was six, Lee was one and a half and I was almost four. None of us really comprehended the magnitude of what had happened. Dad's sister, Aunt Dottie and her husband, Uncle Edgar, had come down from Ohio for the funeral. Grandpa and Grandma Lambert were there from Wellston, Ohio along with Dad's brothers and families. Some of Mom's family was there and most of the miners and their families. They brought food and looked after us kids. After a brief service, Dad was taken to be buried up on the mountain he loved, near Mom's mother, Betsy. Too weak to make the climb, Mom stayed at the bottom with Loretta, while the rest of us went ahead.

The days were gloomy at home following Dad's funeral. The out of town families had returned to Ohio and Mom spent most of her time in bed, not aware of what was going on with us. She couldn't seem to come to terms with the loss of Dad and was not able to care for any of us. The girls tried to take care of everything from cooking and cleaning to overseeing the boys. With no Widow's Pension, Miner's benefits, or Welfare program at that time, they had no money to survive. Finally, exasperated, Franie made Mom understand that she had to look to others for some help. Sending word to Grandpa and Grandma Lambert, they arrived shortly afterward to take us to live with them in Ohio. They already had Great-grandpa Bartoe living with them and adding nine more mouths to feed was a stretch.

"That's what family is for," Grandpa stated rather matter of factly, "I'm sure not going to let all you youngins starve."

Grandma did all she could to help Mom come to grips with the reality of her situation and help her to understand how bad we all needed her. She suggested numerous ways for Mom to support herself and us kids, but Mom couldn't seem to care or grasp the reality of her situation. Grandma had her hands full

with all of us. The girls helped her as much as they could with cleaning and cooking. Being young women, they were quite capable. Grandpa raised peanuts and let Walt and I help him, while Johnny and Doug helped Great-grandpa with the other outside work. Great-grandpa Bartoe was a small, Irish man with a mean temper and having us there didn't help his moods.

Great-Grandfather
Bartoe

Grandma was always on guard to keep him from mistreating one of us. He and Loretta fought constantly.

"Those boys need a whip taken to them," he would beller as he took off after one of them for some imagined crime. Finally, Loretta had taken enough and grabbing the poker from the wood stove, she went after him threatening to beat him if he touched any of us boys.

"They don't need a whipping. They don't know what's going on or what they're supposed to do," she yelled at him.

"Well, girl, you could use a good whipping yourself," he grumbled as Grandma coaxed him back inside the house. She knew Loretta would defend her brothers at any cost. Hearing the commotion, Mom finally realized that we needed to go back home. We left the next day.

Attempting to piece her life back together, Mom baked pies for the local restaurant. Apple, peach, berry, sugar, and sweet potato, everyone in the area knew what great pies she baked. The restaurant sent a boy to pick them up and sold all she could bake. Although, baking pies every day was a lot of work, she could do this at home and never have to leave us three, younger boys. The girls were encouraged and felt things were going to be all right after all. Uncle Edgar and Aunt Dottie came and asked Doug, who was only eight years old, to come with them to Dayton to live. They had two sons of their own close in age to Doug and they felt they could take him to help Mom. He agreed to go and Mom never objected. Franie, having recently turned sixteen, gave up school and took a job with a Jewish couple in Logan as their housekeeper. The couple owned the clothing store in town and could afford paid help. They paid her two dollars a week, which was good money for a sixteen year old. Knowing that the couple across the street was looking for a housekeeper, Franie sent Madeline to apply for the job. At fourteen, she knew nothing about taking care of wealthy people, but she was able to convince them otherwise and got the job. Being only ten years old, Johnny managed to get a job shoveling manure at a dairy farm outside of Logan. That was about all anyone would hire a ten-year-old boy to do. They provided him room and board, which was a big help to Mom. He would hop the train from Logan to Stallings and come home as often as he could to see us. Loretta got a job at the hamburger stand outside of Logan. Everyone that could had found a job to help Mom out and was taking care of themselves. That only left the three, younger boys for Mom to be concerned about at that time. The family believed she could handle that much by herself.

Soon, Mom began dating. An attractive woman, she knew she couldn't take care of herself or even the three of us younger boys for long. She had been too dependent on Dad to be able to make decisions for herself concerning the rest of her life. Without a man to help her, she was lost. Loretta would come home and baby-sit us when Mom had a date, but she hated being in the house alone. Scared to death of the bobcats that roamed the mountains at night, she would pray that Johnny would hop the train and come home on those nights. He seemed to sense when she needed him and usually showed up. He wasn't afraid of anything and Loretta felt safe with him there with us.

Lee and I with friend 1933

Nevertheless, even with everyone working and Loretta helping all she could, Mom decided she couldn't handle the responsibility of us any longer. Without discussing it with our older sisters or any family members, she shipped Walt, Lee and I off to Stalling Orphanage/Detention Home without any warning. Our lives were about to change dramatically.

A plain, red, brick building sitting on the edge of town, the orphanage was unpretentious. Upon entering, we found a huge room with rows and rows of beds and a curtain down the middle. Afraid to ask any questions, we soon found out the curtain separated the boys from the girls. That was as much privacy as there was for anyone. There was a smaller building at the rear, which housed the youngest children. Lee was assigned to that area for sleeping. Everyone ate together in a large dining room where the meals were plain, but filling. On special occasions, the elderly, black lady who did all the cooking would make "chitlin bread." What a treat that was and on Sundays she always made chicken and dumplings. Most of the kids who were there had been caught stealing food. They weren't orphans, but delinquents, and Sunday's meal, they told me, was worth every minute they had to spend at that place.

The days passed uneventfully, if not pleasantly. Life, as we had known it, was mostly harsh anyway. We didn't really know what to expect, so we expected nothing and wasn't disappointed. School was held in classrooms attached to the side of the main building. Walt had started school before Dad had been killed, but was put in first grade with me when the headmaster realized he had not completed the previous school year. He didn't seem to mind and I was glad to have him with me. The adults went about the business of providing for us, doing what needed done and nothing more.

Suddenly, Walt took sick with terrible wheezing, barely able to get his breath. The local doctor was called in immediately to see him and diagnosed him with asthma. Mom was contacted to come and get him. She had to drag him away kicking and screaming. He did not want to leave Lee and me. Of course, getting himself so upset brought on another attack, which guaranteed he would have to go with Mom. The orphanage could not take proper care of him, as they had no facilities or skills to care for sick children.

January nights were cold, especially in the smaller building where Lee slept. Backing up to the gas heater to get warm, he was watching some of the other kids jumping on the bed. Without realizing it, he had backed too close to the heater and, almost immediately, his pajamas were on fire. Without knowing any better, he took off running. As he flew pass the kitchen, Fanny, the housekeeper, caught a glimpse of the terrifying sight. Washing the dishes, she grabbed the dishpan and ran after him. With everything still in the pan, she flung it at Lee's fleeing backside. Being only two and a half years old, the force of the water, dishes and silverware knocked him to the ground, giving the older boys, who had seen him, a chance to put the fire out. Tommy, Lee's best friend, ran to get the headmaster, Mr. Davis, while Fanny tried to comfort Lee and keep him still. The screams and commotion had brought everyone running and we just stood around not knowing what to do or how to help. I was stunned to see it was Lee lying there in terrible pain, but I was afraid to touch him. Mr. Davis carefully lifted him up and rushed out with him. As we all raced to the door behind him, Fanny told us he was taking him to the nearest hospital.

Charlie, one of the older boys, had rushed over to the restaurant where Loretta worked to let her know what had happened. Telling her how Fanny had thrown water on him to put the fire out Loretta was horrified. Believing that water was the worse thing you could do for a burn, she rushed to the orphanage in a rage; sure, that Fanny's actions would prove fatal for her baby brother. Attacking her with a vengeance, it was all the older boys could do to stop her. Finally, under control, she grabbed me and we rushed out, determined to find a way to the hospital. Loretta knew most everyone and she flagged down a car she recognized. Seeing our distress, Tom Johnston, drove us the seven or eights miles to Logan Hospital. It would be years before we would realize that what Fanny had done probably saved Lee's life.

Taken to Logan Hospital, as Stallings was too small a town to have one, Lee was suffering third degree burns over most of his back and hands. By the time we arrived, they had placed Lee on his stomach in a hammock-type contraption. The doctors had placed heat lamps above him to draw out the fire! Although it looked torturous, that was the recommended course of treatment the doctors told us. The lamps would stay on him until a crust had formed. This protected the skin underneath and allowed it to heal, they explained. They had drugged him, thankfully, but that meant we couldn't let him know we were there with him. Forced to return to the orphanage with Mr. Davis, he told me that I could return and visit Lee as often as I wanted if I could get there on my own.

"We don't have anyone to take you over there,'" he informed me, "and besides, he's the hospital's concern at least for the time being." Nothing would keep me from visiting him, even if I had to walk to Logan, I told myself. Loretta assured me she would get someone to take us over in the morning at first light as Mr. Davis dropped her off at the restaurant.

Seeing him the following day made my gut wrench. It was

hard to see my little, red-haired, freckle-faced brother enduring such torment at his young age. I felt completely helpless. I could tell his pain was horrendous and even any slight movement was torture. I made sure to sit on the floor at his face so he could see me and know he wasn't alone. Not being able to turn over, all he could see was the floor and even turning his head to the side was painful. Mercifully, they would put him under with ether when they came to apply dressings, medications, or to clean the wound. Thank God, he was a fighter and I vowed that by the grace of God I would do whatever I could to help him survive this ordeal.

Loretta would give me money from her waitress job to take him ice cream. At least that gave him something to look forward to and I felt like I was doing some small thing for him. Johnny would visit him when he could get away from his job and Doug had insisted on coming down from Ohio when word reached them that Lee had been hurt severely. He was staying outside of town with Mom, so he could visit Lee as often as possible. We would take turns feeding him, talking to him or telling him jokes. Even as young as he was, we all knew he loved singing and we would sing "Black Jack Davey" or "The Wreck of Number 9" to him to lift his spirits. We did whatever we could come up with to keep his mind off his back. My brothers and I kept up our vigil. I missed more school than I attended, but the orphanage didn't seem to care. Whether they understood my concern or it simply didn't matter to them whether I was there or not, I don't know. We didn't care how long it took, we were going to be there to encourage Lee and help him get well. The days dragged on into months as the extremely, slow process of healing took place.

Finally, after more than nine months, the crust was gone, the skin had healed and the itching had stopped. Most of his back and part of his hands were covered with scars and drawn tight. However, he didn't seem to care, his back had healed and he could stand up again. To our surprise, months of lying on his stomach had weakened his legs and he would have to learn to walk all over again. However, with the same determination he had fought the burns, he fought to walk again. Finally, after almost a year from when he had been burned, the hospital was ready to release him. The orphanage refused to take him back, not sure if he was completely well and the hospital had informed Mom she must come get him.

She was living on a shanty boat with Lonny, her new husband, on the Guyandotte River, Doug had told us. I waited with Lee for Mom to arrive. With no apologies for her lack of visits or hugs and kisses as you would expect, we prepared to leave. What a shock I received when she told me I was not going with them. I stood frozen in place as she told me that, instead, I was being sent to a new orphanage in Huntington, West Virginia. The miners supported the Union Mission School and Mom thought I would get better treatment there. Not a word as to why I wasn't going with Lee and her. A different, supposedly, better orphanage was small comfort to me as I watched them walk away. A lady I had not previously noticed approached me.

Taking my hand, she said simply, "You are to go with me." I climbed into the old, black car she led me to without a word. Completely numb, I couldn't even react to the turn of events in my life.

Sitting on the outskirts of Huntington, the orphanage was a three story, brown, brick building. There were separate, dorm rooms unlike the one huge room at Stallings. They were nondescript, neither nice nor unpleasant, simply rooms. The caretakers expressed no emotion toward anyone and just went about their business doing whatever job they were required to do at the time, not much different from Stallings, I thought. They had no time or inclination to know any of us personally and certainly, had no interest in offering comfort, love or support to any of the children housed with them. I was in the first grade again, but I would leave the orphanage to roam around town as often as I wanted. Again, no one seemed to care and no one came after me. You will get a severe beating if they have to look for you for supper, the older boys warned me. That's about all they worry about they continued. I made a point of being back for supper every evening, as I wasn't looking for a beating.

Franie was living with our Aunt Marie in town. Being Mom's baby sister, she wasn't much older than Franie. They shared a small apartment above a clothing store and I would go visit them when I took off from the orphanage. They always gave me some pennies before I left and I would go to the day old bakery and buy treats. I could get a dozen doughnuts for only three pennies and stuff myself. Sweets were unheard of at the orphanage.

Still, this didn't quell the loneliness I was suffering. I missed Lee terribly. We had been through a lot together in our young lives and I didn't understand why he was taken away from me. Why didn't Mom take me home with them? What had I done to make Mom not want me, too? I didn't have anyone to ask and no one offered me any explanation. I spent a lot of time talking to God during my loneliness. I don't know how I learned about Him, but I just knew He was there for me. The only Father I now had, it comforted me to talk to Him. I'm sure He had a role in my leaving that miserable place.

Summoned to the Headmaster's office on a sunny morning at the beginning of summer, I saw a beautiful lady waiting for me.

"Aunt Adela," I shouted, "Have you come to visit me?"

"No, son," was her prompt reply, "I came to take you home with me. Uncle Kenneth and I want you to live with us." Aunt Adela didn't have any children of her own and being Mom's sister she was aware of Mom's current situation. Later on, I would learn that Franie had told her that Mom had come, took Lee home to live with her, and had left me behind to be sent to another orphanage. Being so kind and tenderhearted, she couldn't bear the thought of me still wondering what I had done wrong that I was not wanted by anyone. I was so thrilled to escape that dull, dreadful place I could hardly contain myself.

"Can we go now," I asked. "I don't have to pack. I don't have nothing, but what I'm wearing." The headmaster didn't object and we were quickly out the door. Seeing Uncle Kenneth waiting outside with the car filled me with a happiness I hadn't known for a long time. We drove home to Ashland, Kentucky, but I could have floated, my heart felt so light for a change.

While most of Mom's sisters lived in the coal camps or out in the country, Aunt Adela lived in town. Uncle Kenneth was a policeman for the city of Ashland, so life was a little better for them. They lived in a little, white house with a huge, front porch which seemed to suit Aunt Adela perfectly. She was the typical, southern lady who spent most of her time cooking, cleaning, gardening and caring for her husband. Even though I slept on a pallet in the kitchen, it was clean and warm and for the first time in a long time, I felt cared for by someone. Uncle Kenneth, a tall, well-muscled man, was, surprisingly soft-spoken. Well liked by everyone who knew him, he worked a lot of hours at his job. He was good to me and always treated me well. He was the first man I had been acquainted with who didn't give me regular whippings. I had a lot of respect for him and I tried hard to behave. It was such a joy to spend the warm, summer evenings out on the porch, visiting neighbors and sipping homemade root beer with him and Aunt Adela.

Shortly after arriving, Aunt Adela took me to the doctor's office. It was the first time I had been to a real doctor and I was fascinated. The office was in a small house and had a strange odor about it. Aunt Adela explained that it was the different medicines the doctor used for different sicknesses. A kindly, gray-haired man, he quickly gave me a small pox shot and stated that I was now ready for school at the end of summer.

"I'm going to Grandma and Grandpas first, " I told him. "Aunt Adela promised." Smiling, she took my hand and led me out, reassuring me that I was in fact going for a visit. The shot made me sicker than a dog, however, and for three days, I laid on the couch while Aunt Adela nursed me. I don't remember anyone ever taking care of me when I was sick. Finally, the sickness passed and I got to go visit Grandpa and Grandma Webb, Uncle Kenneth's parents, just as Aunt Adela had promised.

Grandpa Webb ran the mill just outside of town and it was a treat to spend time with him and Grandma. I felt like a regular kid. Grandpa was just an, old country boy, a little shorter than Grandma. He had a white line above his eye that ran diagonally across his forehead. You only noticed it when he removed his cap, which was seldom. Wearing his cap cocked to one side is what caused him to be tanned in that way. Business was very good for him and he had the prettiest set of mules in the county. They had a reddish brown coat that he kept brushed to a sheen. Kate and Hannah were used to turn the water wheel at the mill where he ground mostly corn into cornmeal. Almost everyone in the area brought their corn to Grandpa to grind. He had a reputation of being completely honest and fair to everyone. Although they had some advantages others in the area couldn't afford, Grandpa was never selfish. They had the only electric lights and Grandpa had the only Philco radio. Most of the neighborhood men would gather at his house on Friday nights to listen to the fights and enjoy the fellowship of each other. I was privileged to be allowed to stay up and socialize with them.

Grandma was a large, husky woman, taller than Grandpa. She had a huge, truck patch garden where she grew everything. Green beans, corn, cucumbers, tomatoes, potatoes, okra, you name it and Grandma probably had some in her garden. She spent the summer canning or making jams, jellies and preserves. I helped her all I could, as I was strong for six years old. She was so good to me; I would do anything she asked. I picked strawberries, eating as I went along, but being careful to not trample her plants. Together, we picked cherries, fighting off the blue jays who loved them and the fleas that were attracted to the juice running down our arms while we pitted them. That was not one of my favorite chores, but for Grandma, I would suffer the fleabites without complaining just to be with her.

They took me along to the general store when Grandma needed some supplies. On one occasion, Grandpa noticed me admiring a new Barlow pocketknife. I had never owned a knife of my own and in my part of the world; a knife was a certain kind of badge every father gave his son. Every boy wanted his own knife. Grandpa knew and understood the importance of it and made me an offer I simply could not refuse. If I would sing a solo for him in church the next Sunday morning, he would get me the knife. I agreed to his offer. I was scared that Sunday morning when the minister announced me, but I was determined. I walked up to the pulpit and in my strongest voice I sang, "Will the Circle be Unbroken," for Grandpa. Sure enough, as soon as we got home, he slipped into his bedroom and came out with my Barlow knife. I treasured that very special gift and carried it with me always.

However, all good things must come to an end and so did the summer. School started and I was again in first grade. Not having attended enough the year before, it was decided by Aunt Adela and the school principal, that I would have to go through first grade again. I really didn't care what grade I was in. No one had ever cared if I attended school or not, so the importance of it was lost on me. Besides, I didn't know anyone there anyway. The most special part of school for me was being allowed to play the drums in the toy band. Our uniforms consisted of a baggy, white shirt, red pants, and a red tam. Boy, I thought I was quite the stuff!

The school was close to the center of town and I walked to school every morning. This day was sunny and warm, as the cool of fall had not yet arrived. Just as I was crossing the street to make my way to school, I heard a loud noise behind me. Instinctively, I knew it was gunfire. Without thinking about being shot, I excitedly turned to watch the action. Sirens began blaring as policeman arrived from everywhere. People were running in all directions screaming, the banks been robbed, as shots continued to ring out. Not able to contain my curiosity, I continued walking, looking back over my shoulder. It appeared the robbers were having trouble getting to their getaway car and were firing shots in all directions. All of a sudden, BOOM, I hit the ground with a thud. Not sure if I had been shot or not, I lay still. Not seeing any blood, I realized I hadn't been shot. Instead, I had walked directly into a parked car on the street while I was gawking back at the action taking place on the street. With my head ringing, I picked myself up, dusted off and ran on to school. I knew I was going to be in trouble for being late, but what a tale I had to tell.

One Saturday morning, Aunt Adela, being quite fashionable and well dressed, decided I needed some new things to wear for school. She had already purchased clothes for me when I had first arrived, but she didn't agree with me that I had enough proper clothes. Reluctantly, off I went to the local clothing store with her. Dragging me inside, she quickly spotted and chose the fashionable, but dreaded knickers that so many mothers forced on their sons. Ignoring my protests, she made me try them on. After purchasing them, she insisted I wear them home. I was embarrassed to be seen in those girlie things. Boys wore overalls, not fancy knickers. As soon as we got outside, Uncle Kenneth was waiting with a camera. Oh, no, I thought, not that. I pulled away from her and ran as fast as I could for home hoping no one would see me in that getup. As luck would have it, on the way I passed a huge, reddish, brown mud hill in a vacant lot. Just what I need, I thought, as I quickly climbed to the top. Sliding down a few times I had those knickers covered in mud and torn in the seat and legs. By the time Aunt Adela had caught up to me, they were ruined. Grabbing a sycamore branch, she tanned my hide all the

way home. I was plenty sore by the time she finished, but I pacified myself knowing that I wouldn't have to wear those girlie knickers after all.

Aunt Adela and me in the dreaded knickers

Later on, I realized how wrong it was of me to waste her money and ruin clothes she had bought for me. Begging for her forgiveness, I vowed to try to be a better nephew. She didn't have to be as good to me as she was and I was ashamed. Nevertheless, try as I might, when the school year ended Aunt Adela delivered me to Mom on the shanty boat.

"He's too much for me to handle," she sadly stated, "I tried. I really did try." I was seven years old.

The disappointment of leaving Aunt Adela's was quickly dissipated when I realized all my brothers and Loretta were living on the shanty boat that summer. Mom received five dollars a month for each of us from the state now that the government had started a Welfare program. She had let Johnny come home since Doug hadn't returned to Ohio as of yet. She knew we would not expect much from her or her new husband and having all of us with her was more money for them. Lonny was much younger than her and a good-looking, dark-haired man. Since they had Mom's money, he didn't work much. Having no ambition of his own, he didn't expect too much from any of us. Mom had a new baby girl to keep her busy, so we were pretty much on our own to do as we pleased. Avoiding a beating from Lonny when he got drunk, which was often, was our biggest chore. We quickly learned that Loretta was not afraid of him and was always on guard to protect us from him.

One afternoon we heard yelling and screaming and, suddenly, Lonnie was running through the half-grown cornfield with Loretta hot on his heels, a butcher knife in her hand. None of us attempted to interfere. We knew Loretta could take care of herself and we certainly wasn't about to help Lonnie. Whatever he had done and we all suspected we knew he deserved whatever Loretta delivered. Eventually she returned, but it was more than a week before Lonnie came home. Loretta had packed up and left by then, knowing Mom wouldn't protect her and certainly wouldn't order Lonnie to leave. We would miss her, but we were use to family floating in and out of our lives by then and simply accepted her decision that it was the best thing for her. Lonnie avoided us for the most part after that, not sure, what Loretta had told us, I guessed.

The shanty boat was located about halfway between Chapmanville and Logan on the riverbank. The Great Guyandotte River was a long and deep gorge. It ran past the two towns, which sit on the same side of the river, about seven or eight miles apart. Chapmanville was not really a town, but a cluster of homes built together for safety, fellowship, and community. All the residents felt they were a real town, although they had no stores, churches, or services. Logan, on the other hand, was a large town where everyone went for supplies of all kinds, medical care, to attend church, or to catch a bus to travel.

The river provided many opportunities for adventures, and the five of us were all enjoying being together again. I don't know when I learned to swim, but for as long as I could remember I could swim. Lee, however, needed to relearn, just as he had to relearn how to walk. Although he had developed a fear of the water from the nightmares he suffered after being burned, he was determined to overcome it and swim again. Lonny believed that anyone who lived on the river needed to be able to swim and showing his better side, he took Lee to the "blue hole" and swam out with him holding onto his neck. As he went underwater, he released Lee from around his neck and had him dog paddle around until he resurfaced to get him. In no time, Lee was swimming with the rest of us. He insisted on wearing a tattered pair of swim trunks someone had given him even though the whole rear end was out of them. In his bright, red trunks, with the moon shining, he soon joined us swinging on the grapevines, dropping into the water, and generally horsing around. He spent many an hour, with the rest of us skinny-dipping, at the "blue hole."

One bright, sunny morning, Lee and I decided to journey down the dirt road that lead away from the shanty boat to see what we could discover. After walking a short while, we passed a field with an old, dappled-gray mare just standing in the field eating grass. Glancing at each other, we had the same thought.

"Let's take a ride, "we both said excitedly, as we headed into the field. The old mare didn't stir as we cautiously approached her. Coaxing her out of the field and onto the dirt road, we led her to the edge of the road where there was a fairly high embankment built up. Climbing up the embankment, with the old horse standing perfectly still, I carefully mounted her.

Reaching down to pull Lee onto her back, I told him, "Some horses can be pretty skittish to ride, so be sure you don't kick her ribs." Looking forward to a good long ride, I was totally unprepared for what happened next. Feeling Lee's legs moving before I could stop him, he whooped and kicked the old mare all at one time. Suddenly, there was nothing under me but air and thud; I hit the dirt road with my hind end. Lee was right beside me. Ready to throttle him, after I was sure he was ok, he couldn't hold back his laughter any longer. It was contagious, and I was soon laughing with him. Realizing we needed to get the horse back to the field, we looked around and couldn't find him.

"Probably ran all the way to Logan," Lee laughingly remarked. As we headed back home, we were relieved to see the old, gray mare back in the field we had taken her from in the beginning.

"Oh, well," I said. "She doesn't look any worse for wear.

Guess no harm was done." That, of course, didn't apply to our sore rear ends.

Unfortunately, no matter how many adventures we had as brothers during the day, the good times couldn't erase Lee's nightmares at night. Although Mom was sure they came from him being burned so badly, she had no idea how to help him. She did what she always had done when confronted with a bad situation. Separating herself from the problem, she found a family, the Pridemores, while visiting Madeline, who offered to take Lee to live with them for Mom's Welfare money. She agreed, believing that would solve her problem. Without telling any of us their plan, Lonny and she, took Lee to the long, swinging bridge that crossed the river. Lee would later tell me that it was dusk, dark when they reached the bridge. Giving him a half, working flashlight with vague directions to the Pridemores, they sent him on his way across the gorge alone. Without even knowing whether he had arrived or whether he had even survived the bridge, they returned to the shanty boat.

Morning came and we were told that Lee was gone to live with the Pridemores. We weren't given any explanation or reason and we knew better than to question Mom's decision. What we said wouldn't have mattered anyway. Lee was only four years old and even though I didn't understand, I comforted myself believing he was with a real family. I knew that I might be the next to go, so I decided to make the most of the rest of the summer.

We wandered down to the river as we normally did when we didn't know how to deal with an unpleasant situation. Lee was our baby brother and all of us were sad at his leaving but knowing we could do nothing to change it. Instead, we looked for a diversion. Spying an old number two washtub that had washed up on the bank, Doug decided he was going to make a boat out of it. Scouring around we found two, old, lard can lids he could use for paddles. Climbing inside and sitting cross-legged in the washtub, we pushed him off the shore. Paddling with the lids, he quickly got the hang of it and in no time, he was going from bank to bank. We all were eager to take our turn, but try as we might, not a one of us could ever get it right. Johnny tried by hanging his legs over the front edge, as he was too tall to fit inside cross-legged. He upset as soon as the washtub hit the water. The minute I would sit down, tilt, and over I would go. After being dumped a few times, I surrendered the washtub back to Doug. He made it look so easy, and I decided to be content with watching him, knowing how much he was enjoying himself. He would fly up and down the river for hours on end. If we managed to get a few pennies together, he would go to Logan and buy us whatever we asked for from the general store. It was great fun just watching him.

We swam a lot that summer, but occasionally there was fishing to be done. We didn't fish in the traditional sense very often. Not with a pole anyway. We had never had the opportunity to fish for simple enjoyment. Our fishing was for food. When Mom needed fish for supper, Lonnie would come get us and take us to his fishing hole. As we stood on the bank with him, he would light a quarter stick of dynamite, toss it into the water, and boom; fish would float to the top, temporarily stunned by the noise.

"Go get em, boys," Lonnie yelled, as we jumped in and gathered the stunned fish for supper. We never took out more than Mom could use, as they were a steady supply and we never wasted food. The other fish that had been stunned came around quickly and disappeared into the depths of the river to survive another day. This quick and easy method of fishing was just another example of Lonny's laziness, I reckoned.

Curious, as kids are prone to be, we all knew Lonny hid something down at the riverbank near a sandbar. Early one especially hot day, Johnny suggested we go see if we could find what he had hidden.

"Maybe he's stashing money he's stolen," Doug stated, "or some kind of treasure he found."

"I'm sure I can find his hiding place." I boldly informed them. I had been nearby on a number of occasions when Lonny had visited the spot. Sure enough, we quickly found the spot and started digging. It didn't take long to find a gallon jug in a burlap bag buried just under the sand, at the edge of the water. We instantly knew we had found his stash of "home brew." What a bonanza! Settling down on the nearby sandbar, we started sampling it for ourselves. Nice and cold from having the water running over it, the "home brew" went done easy on that hot afternoon. Passing the jug around, each of us took gulp after gulp. The next thing I knew, I was waking up not sure where I was. Realizing I was on my bed, I had no idea how I had gotten there. Seeing Mom staring at me obviously, not in a real good mood, I said nothing. She promptly informed me that I had been found on the sandbar, drunk as a lord. She had Lonny carry me home, where she put me to bed. I had slept around the clock. My brothers had gotten loaded too, she told me, but apparently, I had drank the largest portion or being the smallest, I was more affected by what I had drank. As I ventured outside where they were, I saw they were still sick and headachy, too. That experience pretty much cured our curiosity about alcohol, at least for the time being, as none of us was enjoying the after effects too much.

Hanging out on the riverbank, we were always looking for something to stir things up for someone. Wearing nothing but bib overalls when we weren't swimming, we always seemed to have a stick of some kind with us. Meandering along, Walt noticed a large, tan-colored bag hanging down from a tree. Before Johnny could stop him, he took a big swat at it. Suddenly, the yellow jackets were on my brothers. Yelling and screaming, Walt, Johnny and Doug, looked like the Keystone Cops running around, bumping into each other as they tried to reach the river. I had been walking a little ways behind them and avoided the yellow jacket's attack. Seeing them, I couldn't keep from laughing like a hyena. Just as the boys started to calm down, the cold water helps stop the stinging, I grabbed my most private parts and screamed bloody murder.

"Oh, my God! " I whooped. The yellow jackets were in my bibs. Ripping and tearing, I couldn't get them off fast enough. I was being stung and stung again. On fire, I finally reached the water. Sinking into the coolness, I waited for the pain to ease. My brothers glared at me without any sympathy and climbing out of the water, they headed for the shanty boat. Knowing they weren't really mad at me, but determined to teach me a lesson, I soaked a few minutes longer. Walking gingerly, I headed to the shanty boat; sure, they had had a good laugh at my expense. Arriving home, I knew better than to complain, in spite of the swelling between my legs. Glancing my way, they knew I had learned my lesson and they were satisfied.

Summer was waning to an end and Mom appeared restless and worried. When Mr. Grayson, the owner of the shanty boat, showed up one morning, we began to understand why. Doug had gone back to Ohio to return to school and Johnny was hinting that he needed to move on. With Lee and Doug already gone, Mom's money had been reduced considerably. Realizing that Lonnie did not intend to pay the rent, Mr. Grayson informed them that they were going to be evicted. With Mom's prodding him, Lonny decided to go ahead and leave. Gathering what little we had we walked to Chapmanville. Madeline had married Garrett a year or so earlier and was living there just on the edge of town. We stopped there hoping, perhaps, Garrett could put Lonnie in touch with someone who had some work and a place to live. He had introduced Lonnie to Mom in the beginning and seemed to know what was going on around town. Johnny chose not to go along and headed for Logan to see Franie, who had, also, gotten married in the past year. Mom didn't seem to mind and he figured he was just as well off there. Although Walt and I went with them, I sensed that it wouldn't be long before I was sent away again.

School had started, but Mom didn't bother to put either of us in school. She had found work, as a waitress at the small restaurant in town and didn't seem to even realize we should be in school. She was distracted most of the time. Lonnie had not found work, but with Madeline's help, he was caring for Sally, our baby half-sister. She had been sick for a while and didn't seem to be getting any better. Madeline was concerned, but with no money and limited medical help in our area, no one seemed able to figure out what was wrong with her. Walt and I tried to stay out of the way and not cause any more work for Madeline, who didn't seem too well herself. On September 29, Sally went to sleep and never woke up. She was barely two years old and we had barely known her. The funeral was brief and Lonny left soon afterwards. Mom grew more despondent as each day passed and began talking about moving. A familiar pattern was forming again, it seemed to me.

Overhearing Mom and Madeline talking, shortly afterwards, I knew Mom was looking for somewhere to send me. If I was going anywhere, I wanted to join Lee, not go to some orphanage again. From what I overheard, that didn't sound like what she had in mind. Madeline did her best to convince her to keep me.

She knew that Mom would keep Walt with her because of his health. I decided I wasn't going to wait around to see if Madeline succeeded in convincing her. Instead, the next morning without a word to anyone, I was off to fend for myself. I didn't want to stay with anyone, even Mom, if she didn't want me. At almost eight years old, I figured I could manage on my own just as well. Besides, I knew Johnny was in the area somewhere and Franie was in Logan.

Aunt Nora, Mom's sister, and Uncle Bernie lived nearby. Although out in the country a little further, I knew I would always be welcome for a visit. Even though they had a small farm, they had too many of their own children to take me in to stay. Nevertheless, I knew she would give me a meal and a warm place to sleep for a night. She was glad to see me and, as was her nature, never asked me any questions. She did insist I stay for supper, as I was sure she would. Aunt Nora was a great cook and supper was wonderful. Vegetables from her garden and hot cornbread made up most of the meal and there was plenty. The topper of the meal was her mouth watering, fried, apple pies for dessert. In the morning, I helped the boys with their chores, to repay Aunt Nora for her kindness. After feeding us a big breakfast, I was on my way, promising to stop by anytime I was close by.

I stayed in the same general area for the most part, roaming from Chapmanville to Logan, being careful to avoid Mom. Sure enough, I was able to find Johnny. Having just turned thirteen, he had given up being a farm hand and had been hoboing and loving it. He seemed to thrive on being foot-loose and fanci-free. He taught me how to hop a train, but I didn't have the courage or the wanderlust to go as far as he did. It did allow me to go to neighboring towns to find work occasionally, but I sensed how dangerous hopping trains was and tried to avoid them. Johnny taught me how to make hobo stew over an open fire. Using any vegetables he could find and whatever piece of meat he could buy or steal for a hint of broth, he just threw it all in any kind of pot he could find. Add some water and salt, he explained, and let it cook for however long you want. In case you aren't offered a meal, he told me, you can always find something to put in a pot. As it turned out, I ate that a lot in the months to come.

Not wanting to be a burden to Johnny and knowing he was getting itchy feet again, I made up an excuse to be on my way. He had been talking about hopping the next train and riding it to wherever it went. Knowing I wasn't ready to do that, I told him I needed to go see Madeline. I knew she would be worried about me, as she had always been my protector. She was going to have a baby, according to Aunt Nora, and I didn't want her to be wondering about me. I needed her to know that I was doing all right on my own.

Approaching cautiously, as I didn't want to run into Mom, I advanced toward Madeline's house. I waited until I was sure she was alone. Seeing her at the kitchen table, she seemed a little under the weather. Making my presence known, she hurried over and ushered me inside.

"What a sight for sore eyes," she exclaimed. "I have worried about you ever since you left Mom."

"I know," I told her. "That's why I wanted to stop and let you know I was alright. You don't look so good, though." Brushing off my concern, she simply blamed it on her condition.

"You're staying the night, aren't you?" she inquired.

"If it's no problem and I'm not in your way," I answered. "I'd love to stay and visit some." That being settled, we sat down awhile and I filled her in on what Johnny had been doing. Telling her about his plan didn't surprise her.

"He has always been like that, "she said, "always on the move. Never satisfied." She tried to keep up with all of us boys, but she had her hands full. Barely sixteen, she was a wife and soon to be Mother. We continued talking, as she told me that Loretta had gotten married also. I was a little surprised to hear that, but realized she probably figured it was the best thing for her since she was on her own and without much education. I helped Madeline prepare supper so I could spend as much time with her as possible. Shortly after eating, I spread a blanket on the floor near her stove and was soon fast asleep.

What a rude awakening I received very early in the morning. As Garrett urgently shook me awake, I was aware of noises coming from the bedroom. Not able to make out what was going on, Garrett explained that Madeline was having the baby. Panicky, he told me it was much too early. He had gotten his mother, who lived next door, to come and help. He was going to try to get to Logan for the doctor. He wanted me to stay with them in case they needed something. Not sure, what I could do, as I had never been in a situation like this, I agreed to stay and do what I could, if anything.

"Make sure the fire stays lit," Garrett yelled, as he ran down the road to find a neighbor with a car. Pacing back and forth, I felt completely helpless.

Before Garrett had returned, his mother came out of the bedroom carrying the tiniest baby I had ever seen. Not much bigger than a grown man's hand, she guessed he weighed no more than a couple pounds. Seeing the fear in my eyes, she told me that Madeline was all right.

"What about the baby?" I questioned.

Too busy to answer me, she motioned, "Give me that shoebox in the corner. I need to make a bed for the baby. We have to keep him warm." Grabbing the box for her, I handed it over and she gently placed him inside. Carrying him to the stove, she placed him inside the oven, leaving the door open.

With a look of shock on my face, I exclaimed, "What are you doing?"

"The baby needs to stay extra warm to keep him alive," she matter-of-factly replied. "He shouldn't have come yet." She seemed to know what to do, as she continued explaining to me. "This is the warmest place in the house and away from any draft. After that, all we can do is pray. He's in the Lord's hands now."

Garrett rushed back into the house alone.

"The doctor is out and no one knows for sure where he is," he offered breathlessly.

"It's ok, "his mother answered. "The baby's here." Suddenly realizing his mother was at the stove, he rushed over to her, stopping abruptly when he saw the shoebox. "It's a boy," she said, "but awfully tiny. I'm doing all I know to do for him. You go see Madeline now." Garrett moved toward the bedroom in a bit of a daze. I knew, that like me, he had never seen such a small baby either and wasn't sure what to do. I simply sat in silence, fascinated at Grandma Bush and her constant tending to the baby. Later on that afternoon, I was allowed to see Sis and know she was ok. I knew I would be leaving in the morning, as I didn't want to cause any more work for her or Grandma Bush. They certainly had their hands full.

Staying close to Madeline's, I worked here and there to keep myself fed and found various places to sleep at night. Sometimes an old shed, under a tree if the weather permitted, sometimes I would be allowed in someone's barn I had worked for that day. I wandered over every couple of days to check on Sis and the baby. She had named him Freddie.

To my amazement, he continued to grow under the watchful

care of Grandma Bush. Too small to nurse, she fed him with a sugar teat she had created. Seeing my concern, Madeline offered to let me hold him during one of my afternoon visits. Eager, but scared, she sat me down and gently placed him in my arms. He was barely there, it seemed, as he still didn't weigh much. Holding him filled me with wonder, at how someone so tiny could fight so hard to survive and was winning. I, truly, saw God's hand at work through Grandma Bush and little Freddie. Thankfully, she was with them, almost constantly, until she was convinced they were both going to be all right. To keep Madeline from worrying about me, I told her I was going to head on over to Logan and let Franie know that she had a new nephew. In fact, I had no idea where I was headed, but Madeline had enough to take care of to not have to worry about me.

Life for me had its good days and not so good days. It was the Depression and many men were out of work. That area of the country was poor to start with and now things were desperate for many people. The coalmines were hard and dangerous work and many men feared them or had lost too many family members to the mines already. Some men tried to survive by farming instead of mining. The land was mountainous though and bottomland sold at a premium. Most families could not afford that and tried to scratch a living out of the side of the hills. Nevertheless, country folks are mostly good and they would let me work for them for a meal most of the time. They knew I had no one caring for me and sharing what little they had was what folks did in my part of the country. Rarely was I paid in money, but a meal and sometimes a barn to sleep in was all I ever asked. That was enough for me.

Hungrier than I had been for a while, I moseyed over to Aunt Nora's. They had a small farm on the outskirts of Chapmanville. Nothing fancy, just barely enough for their family. But, knowing that she worried about me constantly, I tried to stop by and see her every so often. Not wanting her to think I wasn't able to take care of myself, I tried to not let it show how hungry and lonely I was at the time. Aunt Nora was the sweetest lady I knew and I could always depend on her to be loving and caring towards me. She was the oldest of my Mom's sisters and had always seemed more concerned about me than my Mom had ever been. Never one to say an unkind word about anyone though. She shared all she had with whoever needed it, especially me.

After a big hug from her, she sent me off to find my cousins. As usual, she had work to do and knew the boys would be glad to see me. Finding them out back of the barn, we wandered down to the river to see what we could get into. Suddenly, something round and white hit the water right in front of us, barely missing our heads. Wading in, to fetch whatever it was, we saw men across the river hitting the same, small, round, white objects with a stick. Seeing more of them at our feet, we discovered they were a type of hardball. Gathering them up, we approached the men who had come to the fence nearby.

"Those are golf balls," the one man stated. "We use them in our game. "

"How much will you give me for them, "I asked him boldly, knowing they didn't belong in the river and may be worth something.

"That depends on how good they are," the taller man answered. "Like new, I'll give you twenty-five cents. Older ones, ten or fifteen cents and maybe a nickel for beat up ones," he continued.

"A deal, " I quickly accepted.

"Well, let's see what you've got. I can't buy them anywhere else any cheaper, "he stated. Still curious, we asked what game they were playing. "It's called golf, " he told us. After explaining the game of golf to us rather briefly, they returned to the course, re-supplied with balls.

"That was pretty smooth, "Junior commented. "I'm not sure I would have thought of that if you hadn't been here. "Reaching in his pocket he added, "Sure glad you did, though. Made me thirty-five cents. " With forty cents in my own pocket, I felt rich. That was the most money I had ever had at one time in my life.

Heading back to the house, I knew I would be able to be on my way the next morning. Aunt Nora would feel better knowing I had some money in my pocket and I certainly intended on letting her know about our sale. My cousins went off to finish a few chores they had before supper insisting that I just take it easy. As I strolled around the yard, waiting for supper, I noticed her cellar door was opened a crack. Sneaking down the dark steps, I was on the hunt for Aunt Nora's sauerkraut crocks. I was sure she would have some sauerkraut making. Knowing that she always put the cabbage hearts in her crocks, I located them. Sticking my arm down to my elbow, I came out with two hearts. What a treat! I love the hearts of cabbage. That should hold me until supper, I thought, as I carefully placed the cover back on her crocks. Slipping back outside, I was sure I had gone unnoticed. Unbeknownst by me, the brine from the kraut had left a white ring around my arm.

Just after sitting down to supper, Aunt Nora asked, "Paul, have you been in my kraut?" As I hesitated, not wanting to lie to her, she pointed to my arm. Looking down, I knew I had to fess up to her. The entire table erupted into laughter while she threatened to tan my hide if I did it again. I agreed to stay out of it, but I knew she probably wouldn't carry out her threat anyway. I'm sure she knew I probably wouldn't stay out of her kraut either.

Uncle Bernie delivered ice for the Ice Company in Logan and offered me a ride down the road the next morning as he was leaving for work. I rode along for a couple miles, getting out before he turned for town. Not being in any hurry to find work, as I knew I had a little money in my pocket, I strolled along the dirt road unconcerned. Mr. Johnson, who had a small place nearby, called to me from a wooded area.

"Need some help weeding the garden back at the house," he said. "Are you looking for some work?"

Knowing that I needed to take any work that was offered, I called back, "Sure am, be right there." Scampering after him, I knew Mrs. Johnson would see that I had supper after working for them. I had helped them out before and they had always treated me right. The money in my pocket would keep for another day.

"You're a good worker, Paul. I'll let anyone I know that's looking for help know about you if you want," Mr. Johnson stated. "Sleep in the barn tonight, if you don't have any place to go."

Mr. Johnson was as good as his word. I never seemed to lack for some kind of work whenever I needed it. Sometimes I chopped wood for someone's cook stove, some days I picked berries for some of the ladies who made jams and jellies. I hoed corn, helped build a barn for an older farmer, fixed fences or repaired broken doors. I weeded many a garden and picked vegetables for many of the ladies in the area who were busy canning for the winter.

Even old Mr. Whitehead could always be counted on for a little help. His wife didn't approve of him doing for "white trash" or orphans, but he ignored her. Although he would never give me work to do, if he knew I was in his area, he would leave his pocketknife by his smokehouse door for me to cut a piece of bacon to flavor whatever I had found to eat. I think he enjoyed helping me and sneaking behind his wife's back. I would never take but a very, small piece, always making sure to leave his knife spotless. I left it exactly where he had left it and I know he knew how much I appreciated him. Others in the area would let me know where their root cellars were, knowing that I would never take but a small amount and only when I could not find any work anywhere. I made sure I re-covered their root cellars so as not to do any damage. A couple potatoes, apple or turnip could be the difference in whether I went hungry or not. I never forgot the kindnesses of those people to a young, hungry boy.

As I wandered around, I found myself at Aunt Annie's cabin. Married to a full-blooded Indian, she lived deep in a holler. No one in the family was ever sure what type Indian Uncle Luther was and I didn't ask. I had already learned to take people for what they were and according to how they treated me. He was a quiet man, without much to say to strangers or family. Aunt Annie, however, was like a buddy to me.

Having seen me approaching her cabin, as Aunt Annie didn't miss much, she was waiting for me in her porch rocker. Taking a seat on the stoop, I filled her in on what news I had of the family. She cared deeply about the family and appreciated any news. Aunt Annie was quite different from the other women I knew, who did mostly womanly stuff, she was more rugged and outdoorsy. She didn't seem to need much to be happy and was perfectly content being alone in the woods with God, nature, and Uncle Luther. Not unfriendly by any means, she just didn't seem to need a lot of people or the hustle and bustle of town life. She always seemed to know things, like what you were thinking or that someone was approaching. She always surprised me with her intuition.

"You missed lunch, "she commented, knowing I was

hungry. "Got some pie if you want. Should hold you till suppertime."

"I'd love some, Aunt Annie, "I quickly answered. "If it ain't no trouble."

"No trouble, t'all. Come on in, "she gestured, already in the doorway. Before I could sit down, she had a piece of peach pie before me.

"Delicious, "I told her, finishing it off in record time. As we continued our visit, sitting in the kitchen, she was gazing out the kitchen window. I had no idea what she was seeing. Very calmly, she told me to hand her the gun from off the shelf. Knowing to do whatever she asked, I grabbed the gun, being extremely careful. I knew from past visits that her gun was always loaded. She was alone a lot and pretty isolated in the holler. Placing it into her outstretched hand, without her even turning around to look, she placed her elbow on the windowsill to steady herself and fired. Ka-boom, the pistol sounded.

"Go get that squirrel, Paul, "she told me, "We'll have squirrel and gravy for supper tonight, by golly." Rushing out to the tree she had been eyeing, I saw the squirrel on the ground. It had been cleanly shot through the head, slick as a whistle. Amazed at her ability, I grabbed that squirrel by the tail and carried it back to her, waiting in the doorway.

Before I knew it, she had skinned, cleaned, cut-up, and was ready to begin cooking that squirrel. Rolling it around in some flour and salt, she placed it in her big iron skillet with some lard and browned it all over. Pouring some hot water over it, she covered it and started it simmering. Aunt Annie had lost her right leg above the knee, as a young girl, from a thorn that had become infected in her upper calf, Aunt Nora had told me. Unfortunately, gangrene had set in before anyone was able to stop the infection and, with no choice, they had removed her leg to save her life. I don't know about then, but it hadn't slowed her down one bit from what I could see. She moved around the kitchen on her peg leg as quickly as I did on my very own young legs. Asking her about it, she brushed it off.

"You can give up when something bad happens, or you git up and go on, "she stated, as she resumed her cooking. It was clear to me what her choice had been. She was some kind of a lady and I sure admired her.

Smelling that squirrel all afternoon had my mouth watering like a baby cutting teeth. I didn't think suppertime would ever come. Uncle Luther didn't come home by suppertime and, unconcerned; Aunt Annie called me to the table.

"He's out hunting or fishing," she said. "He'll be back sometime," she told me when I asked about him. Squirrel, gravy, biscuits, fried potatoes, greens and more peach pie; I hoped he knew what he was missing. We talked and laughed together all through supper as buddies rather than adult and child. I was full as a tick when we finally quit.

Uncle Luther was a loner who had been injured as a soldier during World War I. Receiving a small pension allowed them to live, as he knew best, off the land he loved and appreciated. Aunt Annie was a perfect fit for him, being so independent herself. We covered up the food that was left over, knowing he would eat whenever he came home, and cleaned up the dishes. Spreading me a pallet on the floor near the fireplace, Aunt Annie rocked and waited. I thanked God for them before quickly falling asleep. I knew Uncle Luther would soon return and all was right in my world that night.

Morning came and sure enough, Uncle Luther had returned sometime after dark. I stayed for breakfast, as Aunt Annie would not hear of me leaving before that, and waving good-bye, I skipped down the lane leading out of their holler.

Thinking about Uncle Luther, as I had not spent much time with him on this visit, I appreciated the simple things he had taught me during past visits. Don't kill any animal you're not going to eat or catch more fish than you need, he had said more than once. Without me even realizing it, he had taught me to appreciate the things nature gives us and to take care of our land. I left with a light heart, knowing that I was always welcome at their door and expected, if I was nearby. I so loved Aunt Annie, her gumption and her simple, peaceful life.

I recalled Uncle Luther's words, as the weather grew colder, and I noticed the animals huddling together to stay warm. Nature will teach you how to take care of yourself if you listen he had told me. The old farm dogs slept by the cows and I quickly realized it was a good place to sleep on a cold night. I would sneak into someone's barn and snuggle up to a sleeping cow for warmth, being sure to be gone by morning's light. On the worst days, when I thought I was going to starve, I would eat some silage out of someone's silo. The cows ate it and didn't die, so I figured I wouldn't either. Thank God, those days were extremely rare.

Having heard that Mom had left Chapmanville to go live in Logan, I wandered over hoping for some work and, maybe, a chance to see Lee.

"Hey, boy," a rough voice behind me bellered. I turned to see Crip Conley, the local moon-shiner motioning for me to come over. "You want a job?" Ruddy-faced with a coarse appearance and booming voice, Crip was intimidating to most folks, but he didn't scare me. He should have been a big man, probably six foot three and about two-hundred and fifty pounds, but he had hopped one too many freight trains. He had gotten his legs cut off just above the knees. "Need someone to make a few deliveries for me," he mumbled, a little quieter now that I had stopped and approached him. Not one to feel sorry for himself, Crip got around with the aid of a small wagon type affair he rode on, pushing himself along with pads on his knuckles. Deliveries in town were no problem for him, but he wanted to hire someone for anything outside of town. Moonshining allowed him to support himself and he paid me five cents for every delivery I made for him. Knowing it was illegal; he knew no one would suspect a skinny, freckled-faced kid, kicking rocks as he moseyed down the road. I was sure that the men I was delivering to would be glad to see me, so I was unconcerned with how rough and mean many of them were reputed to be.

"Sure, Crip, "I answered. "I'm always looking for work."

"Follow me, " he motioned as we made our way to the edge of town. Walking along beside him, I had to admire his guts. Many men would have just quit in his situation. Reaching his place, he placed his burlap bag with the stone crocks over my shoulder, being careful to not break any, and I was on my way. I could make fifteen or twenty cents a week delivering for Crip, which provided plenty of food for me. Moonshining was big business in my part of the country and I gave no thought to the right or wrong of it. All of that goes out the window when you're hungry and on your own. I was just trying to survive, any way I could.

Without realizing that Madeline knew I was in town, I continued my deliveries for Crip. I was at least eating pretty well and sleeping in a cave on the edge of town. Unknown to me, her husband was one of his customers and had told her what I was doing. She was worried about me, knowing that I needed to be in school. She couldn't take me in and make me go, having to care for little Freddie. She felt she had no choice except to carry out the plan she had been hatching. Knowing I was eager to see Lee, she snatched me off the road and took me home with her for the night.

"I'm worried about you," she told me. Nothing I said reassured her and when morning came, she delivered me to Alan Pridemore's house. She was convinced that at least, I would be fed, warm and with my brother. Wanting to see Lee and be sure he was all right, I didn't protest too vigorously. What a mistake that was going to turn out to be.

Lee had seen us coming toward the house and ran out to greet us. He was so happy to see me, as I was him. After giving Lee a brief hug, Madeline was gone. She was too upset by what she had to do to stay and visit. Lee wanted to show me around the place, although there wasn't much to see. We walked over by the river with Lee chattering ninety miles a minute. Sitting on the riverbank, the realization of where I was overcame me and I began to cry. I think Lee sensed how bad I needed him right then and he tried to distract me. Spotting a rabbit running around, he suggested we catch it and cook it for supper. Agreeing to try, since sitting there was not making me feel any better, we took off. Running up and down the hill, the rabbit playing with us, as they do, we exhausted ourselves and my spirits had been lifted a little.

Falling down on a section of new plowed ground, Lee turned to me and said," See, brother, it ain't so bad here. Really, it ain't." I supposed it wasn't, at least I had my brother back with me, but I would soon learn that he was too young to know how bad his life really was at this place.

Without waiting for Lee or me to return, Alan and Oakley had left for her parent's place. Upon entering the house, I was appalled at the filth. Even though everyone I had ever known was poor, they had always tried to keep what they did have clean. This place looked as if no one even lived here. The cracks in the walls were big enough to put your hand through and Alan had done nothing to fill them. I was sure the snow, when it came, would blow in right on top of us. A small back room had a straw pallet on the floor that Lee told me was his bed. The only thing he had to cover up with was a little more straw. An old, fifty-gallon drum that Alan had put in the kitchen provided the only heat in the two rooms.

"I gather coal pieces down at the river, " Lee offered when I asked about the drum. "I got me a bucket hid under the porch to keep it in. Don't want it goin to the Fryes. " Living so close to the mines, there were always some pieces of coal in the river beds. Sometimes, you were lucky and could find some decent size pieces.

"That's sure better than just burning wood all winter, "I told him. Nevertheless, I decided to make sure I kept some wood cut.

Asking Lee about supper, he kinda just shrugged his shoulders and stated he ate what he could find in the kitchen. Looking, I didn't find much, just a little cornmeal and a couple of hard biscuits. Wondering when Alan and Oakley would be home, Lee informed me that sometimes it would be dark before they got back.

"They don't fix you supper? " I asked, knowing they had the Welfare money and food.

"Not most times, "he answered me timidly. Shocked, as Lee was only five years old, I was relieved to be there to look out for him. It was apparent the Pridemores weren't doing much, but I hoped it wasn't as bad as it looked right then.

Alan Pridemore and his wife, Oakley, was just a poor, uneducated, middle-aged couple living in a two-room shack on the side of a hill. They had taken Lee in to get the Welfare money and the food the Welfare office brought once a month, but, it was obvious, Lee was getting no benefit from it. Now they would get twice as much without having to do anything more for me and I was pretty sure they wouldn't. Oakley's parents, the Fryes lived down the road a little ways and they spent most of their time there according to Lee. He had never been allowed to go to the Fryes with them, but I didn't understand why until later.

Alan and Oakley pretty much ignored us, even on the rare occasions they were there. Oakley never made any attempt to be a mother to us, to care for us, clean us or our clothes or cook anything for us. She mostly sat on the porch stoop and stared away. Alan would go into town, occasionally, but never allowed us to go with him. I made sure I did whatever he told me, but it didn't matter. He would come home from the Fryes or from town and grabbing a sassafras bush, he would beat me unmercifully on a regular basis. I never knew what I had done to deserve the beating, so I couldn't correct what annoyed him. He just seemed to delight in the activity it provided him. I hated him and hated seeing him come home, but at least by beating me, he left Lee alone and never once beat him. Oakley never made any attempt to stop him, no matter how often or how severe he beat me. I suspected she didn't care anything about me or maybe beating me meant he didn't beat her. I didn't know.

School was some solace for us. The Pridemores made sure we went to school and the Welfare provided us with shoes to wear and what school supplies we needed. I knew it wasn't Alan's concern for our education, but simply the fact that he knew the Welfare people would check on him before they would pay. Keeping us in school was one of the requirements from the Welfare office and that was one thing they were strict about, at least. Having missed so much school so far in my young life, I was put in second grade with Lee. Being better than two years older, I was embarrassed to be in his class and not very interested in learning. At least it was a little warmer there and no one was beating on me. We seldom had anything to eat for lunch and since I could no longer go out and earn any money for the two of us, we were hungry most of the time. If the teachers knew, they didn't do anything about it and they were about as poor as everyone else, so maybe the didn't have the means to help. I didn't expect anything anyway.

December was approaching and I looked forward to the Welfare people bringing food. I knew they delivered at the first of each month from being with Mom at the shanty boat when they came to deliver. What a thrill when they arrived with a tub of peanut butter, crackers, butter, salt, flour, cornmeal, beans and oatmeal. What abundance, I thought. I was ready for a feast for supper that evening.

Before leaving, the Welfare ladies called Lee and I over to them and wished us a Merry Christmas. Even though, Lee and I knew Christmas was approaching, we had no reason to expect any celebration or even acknowledgement of the season. We had no recollection of Christmas before Dad was killed and we had not had any family to celebrate with since that time. The orphanages we had been in had ignored the season. To our surprise, the older of the two ladies presented Lee and me with two wrapped gifts apiece. Encouraging us to open them, we tore into the small packages, overwhelmed with joy. These were the first gifts we had ever received and we couldn't believe our good fortune. Inside the packages, we found cap guns with extra caps for each of us and a small, cast iron blue racecar for me and a red one for Lee. With tears in our eyes, we hugged the ladies and thanked them from the bottom of our hearts. Christmas was real to us for the very first time.

Watching, to be sure the Welfare people were completely out of sight, Oakley and Alan glanced back at us. With our hearts in our throats, we were sure they were going to take our gifts from us. Instead, they packed up almost all the food that had been delivered and left for the Fryes without so much as a word to us. I was stunned. How foolish of me to think they cared if we had any food. I had thought we hadn't had much to eat because it was near the end of the month when I had arrived. Now, I knew the truth. We were only a way for them to get food and money and not have to do anything for either. The worse kind of people. We were left with a small amount of flour and cornmeal. I guess they knew I would make Lee and I something to eat and Welfare would never know the truth.

Watching them leave, with most of the food, was almost more than I could take. The joy of our Christmas gifts had gone right out the door with them and the food. Sitting at the rickety, dirty table across from Lee, I realized I had to make the best of our situation. He was counting on his big brother and he already felt bad that I got all the beatings. I couldn't let him see my despair.

"We'll make it, little brother, "I told him. "I'll cook us up something we can eat." Knowing that I would have to make what little we had last for as long as I could, I took a small amount of cornmeal and some water and mixed it into a paste. With a small amount of lard I found for the iron skillet, I fried it the best I could. It was something in our stomachs before we fell asleep from the exhaustion that comes with cold, hunger and disappointment.

Some days I got lucky, and Alan didn't come home until we were asleep and I avoided a beating. Most days, I wasn't so lucky. However, I was determined he was not going to break me and make me the mean, no-good person he was to me. Besides,

I had to stay strong for my little brother. After the cornmeal ran out, I would make cakes out of the flour or attempt a poor imitation of gravy. This scenario was repeated each month and we grew more bitter as the days passed.

"Brother, I think we need to make a plan," Lee stated to me one afternoon as we walked home from school. Spring had finally arrived and school would be over soon.

"A plan for what?" I asked, thinking he wanted to run away.

"We're going to have to kill Alan," he stated very matter of factly.

"Yell, I know," I agreed with him. I knew it was eating him up to see me suffer continual beatings at Alan's hand.

"He's going to beat you to death one day if we don't do something soon," he continued.

"I'm sure getting tired of his beatings. But I'm not sure how we can kill him. He's a man and we're just boys," I stated.

"Well, I'm thinking on it," Lee replied, "There has to be someway." We had no thought of the right or wrong of what we were considering. We were just trying to survive and protect ourselves.

"We'll come up with something," I offered.

"It better be soon," Lee answered, as we walked in silence the rest of the way home each alone in their thoughts.

With spring, came some berries in the hills and wild grapes. We would pick what we could to supplement our meager food supply. I seemed to know what was safe to eat and what wasn't. Whether from lessons learned at the hand of Uncle Luther or simply God given instincts He provided me with to keep us safe, I don't know. Cutting a branch from a small, but sturdy tree, I would whittle the point to go gigging for frogs as Uncle Luther had taught me. This was a good time for us as we splashed and waded along the river bank chasing frogs which were usually quicker than us. Once in a while, we would win the contest and have a feast for supper. It wasn't much, but it helped the hunger and with the weather warming, not being cold was a welcome relief and soon it would be warm enough to catch a fish now and then.

Of course, being brothers we occasionally had our moments of conflict. Although rare, sometimes the tension of our situation just got the better of us. I knew as soon as the words were out of my mouth, that I had said the wrong thing to Lee on that spring afternoon. Turning red in the face and chasing after me, I noticed he had stopped to pick something up off the ground. Knowing that even as young as he was, he had a great throwing arm, I tried to make it to the side of the house. Zing, I heard it coming! Ducking to avoid getting hit it the head, apparently that wasn't what he was aiming for anyway. "Yeoww!!" I yelled, feeling the sting in my behind. Lee had reached me by that time, his anger gone, as I reached down to pull the glass protruding from my left butt cheek. A half-moon chunk of a dark colored bottle bottom, it had left a pretty good hole in my behind. Lee helped me wash the blood off and do what we could to stop the bleeding. Plenty sore and bruised, I knew that Alan would beat us if he knew so I made sure to not let on when he was around. I would carry the round, dark, scar forever.

Soon school was out and summer had arrived.

Lee and I were sitting on the riverbank when he turned to me saying, "I've figured it out." Questioning, I looked into the eyes of a little boy I did not recognize. With eyes burning with hatred, he stated to me, "We're going to kill Alan in the morning." The hair on the back of my neck stood straight up as I realized how much he had suffered seeing me be beaten by that man and how much he hated him. His little mind was made up.

"How we going to do it," I asked him.

"We'll find the biggest rock we can carry, "he began, "then carry it up on the roof and hide it. " After some discussion about how we could manage to do that, I questioned him further.

"What are we going to do then? Hope it falls on him? "

Without blinking an eye, he calmly stated, "No, I am going to sneak up there and drop it on him, smashing his head."

"That should work," I said, "if you don't miss."

"I won't," he insisted, "let's find that rock now." We began searching as we walked to the shack. I had never seen him so determined.

"We may have to wait a day or two," I commented to Lee when we couldn't find a big enough rock. "We only get one chance and we have to make sure."

Finally agreeing with me, Lee stated determinedly, "I'll find one tomorrow if I have to go to Chapmanville for it."

I tossed and turned all night unable to stop thinking about what we planned. I prayed like never before, begging God to not let us do what we planned. Lee appeared to be sleeping peacefully, but I was afraid to close my eyes. I guess somewhere in me I knew it was wrong even if I did think Alan deserved killing. Just as the light of day was appearing, I heard voices outside. I strained to hear who was approaching. Bursting in the doorway of our room, I saw a man I thought I recognized. Rubbing the sleep from my eyes, I couldn't believe what I saw. Uncle Bernie and Franie were standing there. Franie was madder than an old, wet hen and began yelling at Alan.

"Oh, my God!" she screamed. "I can't believe you've been treating the boys like this. This place looks like a pigsty. That's where they're sleeping? "She questioned, pointing to the straw pallet. "Get out of my way," she snarled at Alan as she pushed him aside, "C'Mon, boys. You look half-starved. Go with Uncle Bernie. You're not staying here another minute." Alan and Oakley stood in shocked silence, not attempting to respond or stop her from taking us away. Grabbing Uncle Bernie's hands, we were out the door and down the road into town before you could shake a stick at a snake. I, silently, thanked God that He had intervened and we hadn't carried out our plan. We never mentioned it to anyone or spoke of it again.

Arriving at Madeline's house, we discovered that one of the teachers at school had told her that we were being mistreated. Although Madeline had been unable to help us by herself, she had contacted Franie, knowing that her new husband had some family that worked with the Welfare office. Hoping they could help, she had sent word to her and, fortunately, Franie had taken action. Stopping by Aunt Nora and Uncle Bernie's farm on her way from Logan, Uncle Bernie had insisted on coming along in case Alan gave her any trouble. Lee and I didn't care how or why the help had come; only that it had finally arrived.

Taking Madeline along, so she could see for herself that we were ok, Uncle Bernie drove to his farm. We were filthy, yet everyone let us eat before attempting to clean us up. Aunt Nora had prepared lunch for us and what a lunch it was for two half-starved little boys. Pinto beans, fried potatoes, tomatoes from her garden and hot cornbread, was more food than we could eat. Not having eaten a proper meal for so long, we couldn't eat nearly as much as we wanted to at the time.

"That's ok boys, "Aunt Nora assured us, "You can eat some more when you're ready. You'll not go to bed hungry here, that's for sure. "

What a job cleaning us up was for Aunt Nora, Franie and Madeline. Mixing sand with lye soap to try to get our feet and legs clean, I was sure they were going to rub all my skin off my body. Aunt Nora washed our hair with some foul smelling stuff, sure we had lice. It had taken all afternoon, but finally, they were done. With clean overalls on that, Aunt Nora had scrubbed with more lye soap we were released to go and play with our cousins. We breathed a huge sigh of relief. Even though we didn't know what was going to happen to us now, we both felt it had to be better than what we had experienced at the Pridemores. Suppertime arrived and we were able to slow down and enjoy the food and family. Aunt Nora had been right. Going to sleep that night with a full stomach and in a real bed, we felt safe and warm for a change.

Not realizing how filthy we really were, we were surprised when, after breakfast the next morning we were taken back to the number two washtub for another round of cleaning. Franie and Aunt Nora scrubbed us with the dreaded lye soap and sand again. The scrubbings continued for two more days before they were finally satisfied we were clean enough to be acceptable to them. Were we ever relieved. My whole body was pink from the rubbing. Madeline had returned to her family, now that she knew we were safe and in good, caring hands.

Lee and I enjoyed doing chores with Aunt Nora's sons and just hanging around with them. It had been a long time since we had been able to visit our six cousins, who were all boys, except for Thelma. Knowing that we wouldn't be staying with them for long, we made the most of the time we had with them. Aunt Nora fed us well, as usual, and she and Uncle Bernie did all they could to let us know they cared about us. After a few, short days of resting and visiting, Franie informed us we would be going to Logan with her in the morning.

She hated the fact that she could not keep us with her forever, she explained. However, she was pregnant and had a husband that didn't work regularly. Two more mouths to feed would be impossible for her, but she had gotten in touch with her husband's Aunt Goldie, who worked for the Welfare department. Goldie had found an acceptable orphanage in Grundy, Virginia that had been built by a good man who was concerned with miner's orphans and their neglect, Franie informed us.

"It's ok," we reassured her together. "It has to be better than the Pridemores." Goldie arranged for a Welfare agent, Mr. Green, to drive us, as neither she nor Franie were able to make the trip.

Filled with sadness at leaving Franie and apprehensive about what lie ahead, we climbed into Mr. Green's car that September morning and began the trip to Grundy. Perhaps, this would be a new beginning for us. The trip was slow going as we made our way through the mountains. Goldie had told us that Grundy was not too far away, located just over the Virginia border in the western corner of the state. Not having been any further away than Logan, we enjoyed the drive. Mr. Green stopped at a small town along the way and bought a Coney dog and Coca-Cola for each of us for lunch. What a treat!

Lee chattered away with Mr. Green, as he was prone to do whenever he met someone new. A funny sort of kid, I thought happily, as we continued down the road. Lee always made himself feel comfortable wherever he was at any given time. Always one to find some fun in whatever he was doing, he had the three of us singing old folk tunes, such as "Tragic Romance", "Down in the Willow Garden", or "Pretty Polly" as we rolled along. Considering all he and I had been through, those traits had served him well. I simply felt a tremendous sense of responsibility for him and much older than I was, as if I was his Dad. Lee and I had no memory of life with a family or with Dad and Mom. Our occasions with Mom had been brief and usually unpleasant, so we were open to anywhere we could be together and not be mistreated. Maybe at this new place, I could relinquish some of that responsibility to someone more capable than I. Goldie had certainly painted a pretty picture of Mountain Mission School.

Finally, we were there and approaching the entrance, the road split and went right and left around a cattle gate in the middle of the road. Not sure which way to go, Mr. Green chose the road to the right and we drove up to a fairly, large, brick building. The entire area had a pleasant, friendly feeling as we got out of the car with Mr. Green. Immediately, two men appeared at the entrance of the building and greeted us with a friendly hello. The taller and older of the two, introduced himself as Pop Hurley, the President of the school and, turning, introduced Mr. Sublett, as the Dean of Students. Without wasting any time, Pop Hurley turned us over to Dean Sublett to show us to our rooms. Saying good-by to Mr. Green, we thanked him for an enjoyable trip and asked him to let Franie know we had arrived safely.

Explaining that the building they had come out of was the girl's dorm, as well as the Administration Offices, Dean Sublett directed us to a path leading back a holler. As we walked along, he told us that Pop Hurley had started the orphanage/school himself a number of years ago. He informed us they had a dairy farm with approximately twenty-five cows down the road a ways. There were, also, chickens at the farm. This provided milk for the children and eggs for the cook to use in preparing meals. The faculty could have eggs for breakfast if they chose, but there were too many kids to provide eggs for on a regular basis, he explained. Feeling comfortable with Dean Sublett, I asked about the number of children who were here. He told us they had about three hundred children. Most of them are true orphans, he explained, having lost both parents. A few were like Lee and I, who had lost one parent, but because of circumstances beyond their control, were still parentless. Entire families had come to live at the school, he continued.

"Unfortunately, we have to turn younger children or infants away, because we don't have the proper means to care for them. Maybe some day we will be able to," he commented wistfully. Lee and I stared at each other, amazed that there were so many kids just like us at this place.

The boys dorm was a two-story, brick building, not quite as large as the girls, but certainly sufficient. Turning us over to the housemother, he introduced her as Aunt Sis. Noticing our surprise at the familiar introduction, he told us that Aunt Sis was what all the boys called her and she preferred it. A short, elderly lady, she assigned us rooms according to our ages. Being only six, Lee was assigned to the main floor to be near Aunt Sis. The dorm was divided by floors according to ages, which put me on the second floor. Lee and I were separated for the first time in a long time, but with the caring that was apparent here, we knew it would be all right. We felt safe and comfortable already.

After we were assigned rooms, Aunt Sis took us to a large closet down the hall from her office. Inside were rows of overalls, shirts, shoes, socks and underwear, as well as pajamas. She explained to us that all the clothes were placed in this room as they were laundered. We were given two sets of clothes, as we had brought nothing and only had the clothes on our backs. Choosing a pair of shoes for each of us, she kept them, telling us we would get them later on. Not quite sure what that meant, we paid no attention, as neither of us cared for shoes anyway. Offering us pajamas, we politely refused, since neither of us had ever worn them. Heading us down the hall to show Lee where he would be staying, she explained that if you receive a piece of clothing you especially liked, you could keep it in your room rather than placing it in the general laundry. However, if you chose to do this, you were responsible for washing it yourself, ironing it and keeping it repaired. That seemed fair to me.

Accompanying them down the hall, I was not surprised to see Lee excited about where he would be living. Walking a short ways, to the rear of the building we entered a large room with small beds lining the walls on either side. This room accommodated the smaller children who ranged in age between seven and five years. This allowed Aunt Sis ready access to them if they had a need, as she had an apartment type room located at the front of the main level. The day being Sunday afternoon, the room had only a handful of kids. Those who were there accepted Lee without question when Aunt Sis introduced him.

"You'll meet the rest of the kids at supper," she told him. "They're outside playing." I knew with Lee's fun loving ways he was going to be making friends quickly.

Leaving Lee to get settled, I followed Aunt Sis down the hall to the stairway. On the way, we passed another room with more beds.

"I thought all the smaller children stayed back there where we left Lee, " I questioned, as she was easy to talk to.

"Well, some children have a problem at night," she answered.

"What kind of problem? Nightmares, sleep walking?" I continued.

"No, some of the children wet the bed." she calmly answered. "They sleep in this room so I can tend to them easier." Catching a whiff of the room as we passed, I determined, then and there, that I was never going to have to sleep in that room. Even if I had to wake myself every night to be sure it didn't happen.

Climbing the stairs to the second floor, I was pleased to see individual rooms along the hallway. Halfway down, Aunt Sis, turned into a small room with a double bed. Sitting on the bed was a boy about my size.

"E.C.Mullins," he stated as Aunt Sis stepped aside and he got a glimpse at me. "You my new roommate?" he inquired. "Aunt Sis told me you were arriving today." I was pleased that he was so friendly and immediately introduced myself.

"I'll leave you boys to get acquainted, " Aunt Sis stated, noticing that we had seemed to hit it off immediately. "You'll bring Paul down for supper, won't you, E.C?" she called over her shoulder.

"I'll take care of him, Aunt Sis. Don't you worry none." he replied.

Motioning me to sit down on the bed with him, E.C. briefly told me a little about himself and how he came to be at the school. His mother had passed away and, although his father owned a store a little ways down the state, he felt he couldn't take care of E.C. and the store both. Afraid that he was neglecting E.C. and his schooling he searched for help. Having heard good things about the school, he had brought him there. E.C. seemed to be all right with his situation, so I didn't question him any further. In turn, I told him a little about myself and my situation. How my Dad had been killed in the mines and Mom couldn't take care of Lee and I.

"I don't remember him too well," I confided. "I was not quite four years old when it happened."

"There's a lot of miner's kids here," E.C. commented. "An awful lot."

Conversation flowed easily between E.C. and I, with him doing most of the talking. He had surely kissed the Blarney stone. He tried to fill me in on how the school operated. No one called it an orphanage he emphasized. They always refer to it as the school.

"First thing you need to know, I guess," E.C. commented, "is that bedtime is at 8:00. That means you have to be in the bed with the lights out. Aunt Sis is very strict about that."

"What time do you have to get up?" I inquired.

"Oh, don't worry about that," he laughingly stated. "A bell will sound at 6:30 in the morning to wake you. You'll hear it, believe me." E.C. continued with my brief orientation, telling me a little, about many different topics. At almost six o'clock, he jumped up off the bed and grabbing me, we raced out the door. "Wouldn't do for us to be late for supper your first night here." he explained. I hadn't even realized I was so hungry and that the time had flown by so quickly.

Running down the dirt road that led to the girl's dorm, E.C. told me that the dining room was, also, in their building. The girls did the cooking, serving and cleaning up afterwards, so it made sense to have us all eating where they were located. As we entered the dining hall, I saw round tables that looked to accommodate about twelve people at each, placed all over the room. There seemed to be kids of all ages swarming around finding their way to different tables. Everyone seemed to know which place was theirs. The older girls escorted the smaller children. They sat with them so they could care for them as needed. Glancing around, I realized that the girls were seated together on one side of the dining room, while the boys were on the other side. I spotted Lee just as he spotted me. With a grin on his face, he let me know that he was doing all right. Relieved, I knew I could go ahead, enjoy my meal, and get acquainted with the boys at my table.

"Just do what I do," E.C. told me, noticing that I was a little nervous not knowing what I was to do. Everyone grew quiet and each table held hands as Pop Hurley stood up and asked Brother Greenleaf to return thanks. When he had finished, the girls began coming out of the kitchen with stacks of sandwiches piled high on platters. "We get sandwiches every Sunday for supper," E.C. informed me. "It gives the cook a day off." I didn't care what we were eating. I was grateful for anything and the peanut butter and jelly sandwiches tasted mighty good. Each table had a large pitcher of milk and some applesauce to go with the sandwiches and I left with a full stomach. "One things for sure, " E.C. commented to me as we stepped outside. "You won't have to worry about being hungry anymore. There's always plenty to eat here. May not be fancy, but there's always plenty." Although the comment required no response from me, I silently thanked God for that wonderful piece of news. What a relief to know I wouldn't have to worry about Lee being fed anymore.

There was no work to be done on Sundays, according to E.C., so we took our time walking back to the dorm. He pointed out some of the things they took care of through the week. Each boy had a chore assigned to him depending on his age and size. Some took care of the yards, some the garden, some did repairs and most of the older boys worked over at the dairy farm he informed me. There was plenty to do and the boys did all the outside work. The girls did the cooking, cleaning, laundry, sewing and helping with the small children.

"Pop Hurley will assign you a chore tomorrow." he told me confidently. "I'm sure of that." Meeting some of the other boys along the way, he made sure he introduced me to them. "Most everyone is friendly here," he said. "We're all in the same boat."

Lying in bed that night, my head was spinning with all that had taken place in that one day. I thought about Franie and how worried she was to see us leave. I hoped Mr. Green had let her know we had arrived safely. I wanted her to know how much better this place was than where we had been. I thanked God for her and Goldie having arranged for Lee and me to be here. I felt confident that our life was going to be better here than it had been anywhere else we had been previously. When the lights went out at eight o'clock, I quickly drifted off into a peaceful sleep. God was surely watching over Lee and me.

Waking up before the bell, I glanced around to be sure I hadn't been dreaming. Yep, E.C. was lying there next to me, just beginning to stir. Not sure what the day would bring, I was sure E.C. would direct me to wherever I needed to be. He had turned out to be a really decent guy and I was hopeful that he would become a good friend as well. Just as I snuggled down for a few last moments, the bell sounded. Rolling out of bed, we pulled on our overalls and headed to the stairway. Boys were pouring out of the rooms, two by two, making their way downstairs. Stopping by the outside door, I saw each boy reach down and pick up a pair of shoes from the rows of them along the wall. Questioning, I glanced at Aunt Sis, who was holding out the pair she had chosen earlier.

"We always wear shoes to chapel and school, but we don't wear shoes in the dorm," she said. "They make too much noise and cause too much cleaning. You will remove them when you return each day." she continued. I thanked her for the shoes but, since I hated wearing them, this was a rule I certainly wouldn't mind observing.

Breakfast was conducted the same as last night's supper. The only difference was Pop Hurley requested one of the older boys to say grace. The girls delivered oatmeal and fruit to each table in the same manner as before. Milk and sugar was on each table to use, as you wanted. E.C. had been right, there was plenty to fill you up. Asking E.C. about the prayer, he informed me that Pop asked different people at each meal. He wants everyone to feel a part of the school was E.C.'s opinion.

Finishing breakfast, we headed over to the Administration Building where chapel was held. E.C. had told me the night before that chapel was held every morning before school. Pop Hurley belonged to the Church of Christ and the orphanage had been set up based on those beliefs. The church helped support the school and Pop felt religious education was an important part of our schooling. Although I had talked to God often in the past, especially when I was scared or lonely, I had no recollection of attending church. I suppose I was too young when Dad had taken us to remember. The chapel filled quickly with the boys on one side and the girls on the other. This seemed to be a common practice. Pop Hurley took the pulpit and everyone grew quiet. Opening with a prayer, he then asked Brother Greenleaf, a visiting minister from Grundy, to lead us in singing, "I've Got a Mansion." Pop Hurley read some from the Bible, and then spoke for a few minutes, teaching us the Bible lesson. After closing with another prayer, he sent us off to school. I left the chapel with a strangely, peaceful feeling.

As E.C. and I walked to the school, I spied Lee hanging back a little from his group. Seeing Dean Sublett appear, E.C. left for his classroom. Dean Sublett escorted Lee and me inside as I told him we had missed a lot of school.

"Most of our children have," he responded. "What grade do you think you should be in at this time?" he inquired. I suggested third grade and without further questioning, he showed us both to the third grade classroom and introduced us to Miss Spring, the teacher.

Miss Spring was an attractive, country lady of about thirty-five years. She thoroughly enjoyed teaching according to Dean

Sublett. She was pleased to have two new students, she told us, and welcomed us without hesitation. Assigning us desks, Lee was placed in the front of the room, as he was much smaller than I was. I think she knew I was embarrassed to be in the same grade and she gave me a desk toward the rear. As the class filled up, I began to not feel so out of place. There were boys and girls of various ages in my classroom and I realized that Dean Sublett had been right. There were plenty others like me, who had not been in school regularly. Calling everyone to attention, we stood up and recited the "Pledge of Allegiance," being lead by Miss Spring.

"Now, open your readers," she stated and school began in earnest.

The school was a separate building made of rough-cut wood. It sat to the left of the administration building with a sidewalk leading to the main door. A plain, one-story building, the school contained one classroom for each grade. All the teachers lived on the grounds, having rooms in the administration building. All but one of them were women, with the only male, teaching the twelfth grade. I soon learned how dedicated they all were to the children and the school. They really did care about everyone of us.

After a half-hour break for lunch, which was handled the same as every other meal had been, school continued until 3:30. Miss Spring instructed me to wait outside for Pop Hurley. Lee joined me out there, but we didn't have to wait long. Pop was approaching as we started down the sidewalk. Acknowledging Lee, he told him he would not have a regular chore just yet. He was expected to help as asked, he explained to him, but he was still too young for a regular chore. He would be assigned one when he turned eight, Pop explained to him. Sending him on his way, Lee caught up with some friends his age. Pop reminded them to be sure and report to Aunt Sis when they reached the dorm. The younger children were required to do this after school.

"Come with me, Paul," Pop said. "You appear to be a strong, healthy, young man."

"Yes, sir, I believe I am," I quickly replied. Not afraid of hard work, I didn't want him to think I minded any chore he wanted to assign me. Walking over to a large concrete slab in the ground, I had no idea what was there.

"Follow me," Pop motioned me, as I noticed a stairway leading down to something in the slab. Reaching the bottom, we had entered a huge, solid, concrete room. "This is the coal furnace." Pop explained. "This heats all the buildings in winter," he continued, pointing to the furnace on the backside of the room.

"All the buildings?" I questioned. I did not understand how the heat could get everywhere.

"Yes, all of them. There are pipes buried under the ground, coming from here. They go to each building and the heat goes through them," he patiently explained, apparently pleased that I was curious. "Someone needs to fire the furnace every day when cold weather comes," he stated. "I'm sure you can do it. We'll teach you how when the time comes."

"Yes, sir," I answered. "I'll do my best." I knew this wasn't a request or suggestion and I only hoped I could do what Pop had asked.

Leaving the furnace room, Pop told me I would be helping out in the gardens and fields until cold weather made the furnace necessary.

"You can go on back to your room for today," Pop stated smiling. Relaxing a little, I glanced up at him, not sure if he was finished. "Tomorrow's soon enough to start working," he said.

"I'll have one of the older boys show you what to do tomorrow after school."

"Thank you, Pop," I said and slowly walked back to the dorm. I was sure I could do any chore that was asked of me. This was a good place for Lee and I, and I wasn't about to do anything to cause them to send us away.

Supper was pinto beans, boiled white potatoes, sliced tomatoes and cornbread. Although, I didn't drink milk, it was always available for those that did, as well as water, which I chose. E.C. told me we had the same food, for the most part, every day. The vegetables and fruit vary according to what is growing in the garden at the time he explained, but you can always count on beans, potatoes and cornbread being served. After all the hungry days, I had known in the past, I sure wasn't that particular. I was grateful for any good, hot meal and didn't much care what it contained.

As E.C. and I left the dining hall, another boy joined us on the path.

"Paul, this is Mose Belcher," E.C. stated. "He's a good friend of mine."

Sticking out my hand, "Paul Lambert," I told him."

"You new?" Mose inquired, as he shook my hand firmly.

"Yes, just got here yesterday," I responded.

"He's my new roommate," E.C. explained. "Got a little brother here, too." We had reached the dorm by then, but since it wasn't time for lights out and they both had their chores done, we settled down by a big tree to continue talking. Mose was twelve and quite a bit bigger than E.C. or I. A friendly sort, he made me feel comfortable with him immediately. Mose began giving me a brief history of the school and Pop Hurley.

When Pop was only ten years old and called Sam at that time, his father died, Mose began reciting the story, as if he'd

71

told it many times before. He went from house to house in the mountains of Eastern Kentucky searching for work in exchange for food. Sleeping in a cave, with the barest of clothes, he piled up leaves to try to keep warm. He was very cold and scared most of the time. One night the sound of the catamount kept getting closer and closer. He cried out for God to save him from the catamount. He made a bargain with God and promised that if He saved him, he would build a safe place for boys and girls like him when he grew up. Mose glanced my way, to be sure I was paying attention. Seeing I was listening closely, he continued. Well, Sam did survive and grew up to become a very successful businessman even though he had never attended school. Having married, Jane, as she was called by him, at twenty-two, she taught him to read and write. He had forgotten his promise to God. One day at his office in the courthouse in Grundy, a little, poor, homeless boy came in and asked him to take him home with him. Telling him he already had seven children of his own and nine others he had taken in, he sent him away stating he had no more room. When he left his office, he spotted the child sitting on the steps crying and God reminded him of his promise of so many years ago. Taking the child with him, he immediately went to his lawyer and completed all the paperwork to start the school. It was called Grundy Academy at that time, Mose stated. That was back in 1921 and he got Dr. Hopwood and his wife to come and set up the school. He had retired from Milligan College and ran the school as long as his health allowed. Pop and Mom Hurley moved onto the campus at that time and put all they owned into the school. Pop became the President, with Mom Hurley doing whatever was needed of her.

"Then he was like me," I told Mose and E.C.

"He was like all of us," they responded quietly.

Mom and Pop Hurley

After a few moments of letting the story sink in, Mose stated, "Everyone respects Pop Hurley and he's known all over the state."

"Don't be fooled, though," E.C., added laughingly, "he takes care of everyone here, but if you do wrong, he won't hesitate to give you a whipping."

"Yep," Mose added, "he believes in discipline. I know that from experience," he chuckled, rubbing his bottom for emphasis.

"What about Dean Sublett then?" I questioned. These two boys seemed pretty well informed.

"Oh, Dean Sublett is married to Pop's daughter. She's one

of our teachers and really nice. However, believe me, he isn't afraid of using the paddle either. You have to break one of the rules, be disrespectful, or do something dangerous before either of them will resort to the paddle, though." Looking a little concerned, as I wasn't sure what all the rules they were discussing were, E.C. noticed.

"Don't worry," he assured me. "You'll know all the rules by week's end."

Even though we had been talking for quite awhile, I had a question I needed answered. "The little boy at school, with the braces on his legs? I see him with Pop a lot. Is he theirs? " I asked.

"Oh, you mean Timmy. Well now, he's a good example of how Mom and Pop are. Their kids are grown, but when Timmy was left here, they knew he would need special attention so they took him in as their own. He had polio, that's the reason for the braces," Mose explained.

"Oh," I replied, as I couldn't think of anything else to say. It was getting late, so we made our way to the dorm, stopping to remove our shoes before we climbed the stairs and headed for our rooms. "Good to have met you, Mose," I told him as we stopped at his room. "Thanks for everything."

"Just a minute, Paul," Mose stopped me as I headed for my room. "Want you to meet my roommate. He's a good guy you'll want to get to know, I'm sure." Mose commented as he motioned to a blond haired boy in his room. "Paul, this is Don Absure," he introduced us.

"Paul Lambert, "I stated. "Glad to make your acquaintance."

"Me, too," Don replied. Reaching our room, I hadn't expected to be so tired. A lot had happened in just one day and I had learned an awful lot. I knew I still had a lot to learn, but I was sure with E.C., Mose's and now, hopefully with Don's help, I'd learn all I needed to know fairly soon. Quickly, I fell asleep

Pop had been as good as his word and the next afternoon, Mose showed up to take me to the garden to work until supper. I was glad it was Mose and the work wasn't anything I hadn't done many times before. After showing me where and what I was to do, Mose went on to take care of his own chores. Steadily working, I thought about the school. Having clean clothes everyday, good, filling, hot food three times a day, a comfortable, warm bed to sleep on and someone to guide and teach you. What more could I possibly ask for, I reasoned. E.C. and Mose, as well as other boys I had already met were an added bonus. I knew Lee was doing all right and making friends. The routine of each day would soon be familiar. It felt good knowing that I was doing my part, now that I had a chore of my own.

Before I knew it, Saturday had arrived and with it, no school. Crawling out of bed at the 6:30 bell, I looked forward to what the day would bring. E.C. had told me that Pop or Dean Sublett would have some job for us to do after breakfast, but that most Saturdays, we would be finished by lunch. After that, we would be allowed to go into Grundy, if it was our week, or do whatever we wanted. The boys and girls weren't allowed to socialize together, so we could go one Saturday to the movies or whatever we wanted to do in town and the girls went the next. E.C., Mose and I walked over to breakfast with the rest of the boys. After eating, Dean Sublett gathered us together and we headed to the dairy barn. We spent the morning cleaning out the stalls, shoveling manure, feeding the cows, and generally making sure everything was in tiptop shape. Satisfied, as we headed back to the school for lunch, Dean Sublett released us for the afternoon to do what we wanted.

"Remember," he told everyone, "if you're not back for supper, you will go to bed hungry."

Although, I had no money to spend, I decided to accept E.C., Mose, and Don's invitation to go into town to see what was there.

"Where'd you get any money?" I inquired. The boys explained that there were people from town who came to the chapel on Sunday for church service. They would pay you to do work for them some of the time. You can, also, gather walnuts or hickory nuts in the woods outside the school and sell them for some spending money, they told me. In the spring and summer, you can pick berries up in the hills. There's always someone in town who will buy them they explained. Pop allows us to do that, as he believes its good to have your own money and not have to spend it on food they continued. Never one to turn down an opportunity to earn some money, this was great news to me.

Grundy was down at the end of the road that led to the school. Deciding to be my guides, they showed me the Lowe's Movie Theater where you could see a movie on Saturday afternoon for nine cents. This was the favorite thing to do for most of the kids. On down the street was a soda shop and restaurant, and, of course, a grocery, bank and newspaper office. Maybe when you're a little older, you can get a paper route Mose told me. I determined that I would soon be earning some money for myself and be able to join my friends at the movies. Refusing to go to the movies without me, we four just wandered around town. Don had turned out to be as good a guy as Mose had said. His father lived in Akron, Ohio and he had been sent to Mount Mission when his mother had passed away. That was about all he had told me, but it was all I needed to know. I never pressed anyone for any more information that they wanted to give me. He treated me all right and I liked him immediately. Even though I had only been at the school a week, I was beginning to feel comfortable with my new pals and this new area. It seemed as if everyone made every effort to make you feel welcome and a part of things going on.

As the days became weeks, and September became October, Pop informed me it was time to start up the furnace. Since it had been Mose's job before I came, he sent him to instruct me. I couldn't imagine how big a fire would be needed to heat the school, the girl's dorm and the boy's all at one time. I did know, however, that I was going to do this job one way or the other. I would soon find out that it took a lot of fire and a lot of work.

"To begin with," Mose explained, "you have to gather up some old newspapers and kindling and place them inside the furnace. You light that with a match and when it's burning pretty good, you add the smallest pieces of coal you can find." Pop had already had a load of coal delivered, which filled the cement floor to the right of the furnace. "When that is burning good, you add some bigger pieces of coal, spreading the fire around the entire bottom of the furnace." Mose continued, as he showed me what to do. The interior of the furnace that needed to be filled was about eight feet wide. "Once you have a good base, you can just start shoveling the coal in until you think you have enough to keep it going for awhile," he stated. "Just be careful and not add the bigger pieces too fast or too soon. You don't want to smother your base, believe me," he chuckled. "You have to remove everything and start over if you do," he added, "and you really don't want to do that."

I had watched him carefully and asked, "How long does it take to burn down?"

"That all depends on how cold it gets," he answered, "Later in the winter, you may have to sleep here to be sure it doesn't burn out. This time of year, you probably won't have to keep in going every day. If the days are warm, Pop will let you know if he wants it burning or not for the nighttime." I was sure I would have more questions, but I couldn't think of any more just then.

"I think I understand," I told Mose.

"Oh, you won't have any problem," he answered. "You're plenty strong enough to shovel all the coal you need. That's about it."

I was fortunate that first October, as it was extremely mild. More warm days than cold ones allowed me to learn my new job without a lot of pressure. Pop usually had me start up the furnace after supper as the sun was setting to keep the chill out of the buildings overnight. By the end of the month, I was pretty adept at what I was doing. Maybe my cockiness contributed to Don and I having a knock down, drag out fight shortly after getting to know him.

Hanging around outside the dorm, the four of us were just acting up, when all of a sudden, KERPOW! I had said something Don took the wrong way, I guess. That blow caught me on the jaw and I instantly reacted with a punch myself. Still on our feet, swinging like mad, I realized he was quick as lightening, as I ducked a punch. We were going toe to toe, matching each other's punches with frightening speed and intensity. Not even sure, what had happened, I was determined to not let him whip me and he seemed as determined. We both landed on the ground with him on top of me, then me on him and vice versa. Struggling to get back on our feet, we both finally realized neither of us was going to give up. We stopped and stood, fists clenched, just staring at each other, not sure what we were doing or why.

"Well, you boys about done?" Mose asked. That seemed to make sense to us and we both plopped down in the grass together. Mose and E.C. just watched us to be sure we were ok. Shrugging, we let the moment pass with nothing more said. We soon joined in the conversation as if nothing had ever happened. We later returned to the dorm, the fight forgotten. Although no words had been exchanged, we both knew there were no hard feeling between us and was relieved.

Don Absure

My birthday passed with no one noticing. That was not surprising to me, as I had never had it celebrated. It was just another day to me, nothing special. Things were going along pretty well anyway. School wasn't so bad and Miss Spring had mentioned to me that she thought I had quite a head for figures. This was the first compliment I had ever had at school and with her giving me a little individual attention, I got my first ever A+ in math. It was my first A+ in any subject and I was rightfully proud. Miss Spring, who I adored, told me she was pleased to award it to me, since I had worked hard. I planned to continue studying hard for her so she wouldn't be disappointed in me.

I had been able to do a few odd jobs for some folks from church and had a little money for movies and occasional treats. I had discovered there was always a way to earn money for any of us that wanted to work, just as my friends had said. Loretta's words about Dad's beliefs would run through my head any time I felt like slacking off. She would have been glad to know that the lessons from Dad she drilled in my head at the shanty boat had stuck, I'm sure.

By December, I was firing the furnace every morning before breakfast and checking it before school started, making sure I had a good-sized fire burning. Depending on how cold the day was, that would last until school was over. It only took a few minutes to check on it and add coal if I needed to. Miss Spring allowed me to leave class long enough to take care of it, if it was necessary. I would check on it every few hours after school and then bank it before going to bed at night. Banking it meant shoveling a large amount of coal into the furnace, throwing it as far back as possible, and continue adding more coal. Without smothering the fire, I added all I could to keep the fire going all night. On very cold nights, I slept in the furnace room so I could tend the fire all night as needed. I was getting use to the routine and was always aware of the importance of my job. Everyone depended on me to stay warm and I had been cold often enough that I made sure they never were.

There were lots of fun times with my friends that first fall, also. It wasn't all school, work and routine. Pop Hurley made sure every one had some time for play and relaxing. Although that many kids was a huge responsibility for him and Mom Hurley, it seemed to me, he never forgot that we were first of all children. I guess I noticed that because the other orphanages Lee and I had been in had treated us as if we were wooden soldiers with no hearts or feelings. Most Saturday afternoons we had free and spent them at the movies. Don had become my very best friend, strangely enough, and I was seldom without him, E.C., and Mose. We would take Lee along with us to the movies most of the time. He loved them more than any kid I had ever seen. For only nine cents apiece, we got to see a newsreel, two cartoons and a double feature film. The movies were mostly cowboy movies and for an entire afternoon, we would be out in the old West fighting outlaws or Indians. Even though I had to keep an eye on the furnace on the weekends, too, I was still able to enjoy myself with my buddies and our Saturday afternoon escapes. Sundays would usually find us in the woods gathering nuts to sell, searching for caves in the mountain, playing in the snow if we had some, or hanging out with buddies in the furnace room where it was warm.

As Christmas approached, there was a buzz of excitement around the campus. Having only the one recollection of Christmas with the Welfare ladies when we were at the Pridemores, Lee and I had no idea what to expect. During Saturday morning breakfast the week before Christmas, Pop told everyone to meet in the auditorium where chapel was held after eating. Although E.C., Mose and Don knew what was going on, they didn't spoil it for me. Rushing over to the auditorium, we noticed four of the older boys dragging a tree down from the mountain behind the school. As they brought it into the auditorium, Pop and Dean Sublett, who had been preparing a stand, took it and attached the stand. I watched in silence as they set it upright.

"A real Christmas tree," I muttered to E.C. "Isn't it beautiful."

"You just wait," Mose stated just as Pop called everyone to the tree.

"Gather around," Pop told us, "We've got to get our tree decorated." Aunt Sis, Mom Hurley and all our teachers appeared out of nowhere with bowls of popcorn and berries.

"Let's get to work," Mom said, "we've got to get this strung before we can put it on the tree." Those who had done that before showed the rest of us how and soon we were all at work. Dean Sublett and some of the taller boys, Mose included, strung the lights on the tree, as some of the girls began singing Christmas carols. The morning flew by in a beehive of activity.

The girls left to prepare lunch as we started placing our strings of popcorn and red berries on the tree.

Stepping back to admire our handiwork, Don asked Pop, "Where's our star for the top?" Apparently, he knew from Christmas' past, that the tree wasn't complete just yet.

"I haven't forgotten," Pop, answered, "But it'll wait until after lunch." Corralling, all of us still there, he escorted us down the hall to the dining room, knowing we really didn't want to stop to eat.

We raced through lunch, since all of us were eager to get back to our tree decorating. Don, Mose, E.C., Tommy, and most of the other boys at my table had been here for past Christmases, so they understood my anticipation. Not wanting to spoil it for me, they said nothing about the upcoming celebration. We returned to the auditorium as soon as we finished, but Pop wouldn't continue until the girls had a chance to finish cleaning up from lunch and had joined us. Dean Sublett climbed up the ladder to place the star Pop had given him on the top of the tree. He made sure he placed it so the lights at the top shone on it.

"All ready, Pop," he called out, "let's have some lights."

Plugging them in, the tree was instantly transformed. Ohh's and ahh's sounded throughout the auditorium, from the youngest child to the oldest adult. My first ever Christmas tree! I don't think I had ever seen anything so beautiful. All three hundred of us just stood and stared, alone in our thoughts. Mom Hurley suggested we sing a few carols in celebration before we parted for the afternoon. What a joyful sound we made as we all sang together.

I had to check on the furnace, so my buddies followed along. It was always warm down there and no one had any inclination to go into town at this hour even though it was Saturday. We all had a contented, peaceful spirit about us that afternoon and I just listened as the boys reminisced about other Christmases here at the school.

"Some of the town's people and churches around the state make donations to the school during the holidays," Mose explained to me. "They want to help make sure we have a nice Christmas."

I had no idea what that meant, so I asked, "What do you mean, a nice Christmas? Do we get candy or something?" Looking around among themselves, they chose to tell me nothing.

"Just wait until Christmas morning," E.C. stated, "it'll be better that way." I sat wondering, as they smiled at each other sharing their secret.

Just as I was convinced the week would never pass, it did at last. I had looked forward so eagerly to the big day. Christmas morning had arrived! The week had been filled with the grownups always secretly busy and my buddies completely closed mouthed. E.C. and I were out of bed at the first sound of the bell, dressing in the nicest clothes we had available. I rushed out ahead of E.C., as I needed to fire the furnace before breakfast. Making sure I had a good fire going, I met E.C., Mose, Don, and the others for breakfast. I could barely choke down my breakfast, I was so anxious to see what the day would bring. We made our way down to the auditorium, where the Christmas tree was lit, to take part in our Christmas service.

Pop Hurley began the service with a prayer, and then asked Dean Sublett to lead us in singing "Oh, Little Town of Bethlehem." It was a good selection, which lead into some of the children performing the Christmas story. I had a vague memory of the story from somewhere in my past that I couldn't quite place. Seeing the children in costumes, with a stable and manger on stage, really brought to life why we celebrate the season. Baby Jesus was a real baby, borrowed from one of the ladies who was visiting from town. That made the whole program even more special. They finished the program with all of us joining in singing, "Joy to the World." Pop completed the service with a few words and a final prayer. It was a very moving experience for me.

No one moved when he finished and I followed their lead. Those of us who had never experienced Christmas at the school were anxiously squirming around and watching the others for some clues. Pop called all the adults to the stage and without waiting any longer, began calling the children forward row by row. As was appropriate, I guess, he started with the youngest working his way through every single child in the place, calling each one by name.

Even though I tried to be patient and act nonchalant, I was thrilled when our row was called. Approaching Pop, I realized how much he was enjoying himself, too. Our usually stern disciplinarian was showing a softer, happy side of himself as he handed me a brown, paper bag and two wrapped gifts.

"Merry Christmas, Paul," he said, "glad you're with us." I could barely get any words out for my excitement.

Finally, I mumbled, "Merry Christmas to you, Pop and thank you so much. I'm glad to be here, too."

Trying to contain myself until I got back to my seat, I couldn't resist peering into the paper bag he had given me. Inside, I saw an orange, an apple and lots of hard tack candy on the bottom. Just the smell made my mouth water and I pulled out a piece of candy to suck on while I opened my gifts. Don, Mose, and E.C. were as excited as I was by this time, after all, they were still young boys, too. Tearing the wrapping off, I found two pair of warm socks and new underwear in the first box and a good-sized racecar in the second.

"Most everybody gets something to wear and something to play with," Don commented, happy with his gifts.

"I'm happy with this," I said, "it's more than I ever expected. This is the best Christmas I've ever had."

Finding Lee, as Pop directed us to the dining room, he was as happy as I was and excited to show me his gifts. Babbling non-stop all the way to the dining room, he was especially thrilled with the Christmas play. Loving movies as he did, that didn't surprise me too much.

"Maybe I can be in it next year," he said, wistfully.

"Maybe you can," I answered him, happy we were here together celebrating Christmas.

Before we even reached the dining room, I could smell things I hadn't smelled here before. Knowing the girls had been in the auditorium with us, I didn't know what I smelled or was cooking. It certainly smelled delicious, though.

Reaching my table, Mose told me, "Ladies from the church and some from town come and cook Christmas dinner for us so everyone can enjoy the day," as if he had read my mind. Before I could ask any more, Pop rose and said the prayer himself, thanking God for all our blessings. I silently said one of my own, since I had an awful lot to thank Him for myself. As soon as he finished, ladies appeared everywhere, serving turkey and dressing, mashed potatoes and gravy, green beans and corn, sweet potatoes, cranberry salad and hot rolls. I thought I would die! I had never had such a meal, even at Aunt Noras. The joy of Christmas was on every child's face as we feasted. Sitting back, stuffed, the ladies returned with trays of Christmas cookies for dessert! It had been a wonderful day. So much more than anything I could have imagined in my wildest dreams. The joy and love was so strong you could see it, feel it, taste it, smell it. It permeated everything.

Returning to the dorm with my buddies, I thanked them for keeping the day a secret from me.

"You were right, E.C.," I told him, "It was better this way." Everyone was happy and content and just hung around the dorm, visiting with each other and examining our gifts. Not wanting to leave, I knew I had to go tend to the furnace.

"I'll go with you," Don said.

"But I may have to sleep there tonight," I told him, "you don't want to do that."

"It's ok," he said, "it's no fun to be alone tonight." As we stepped outside, I knew God had smiled on me. It was not very cold at all and I was able to fire the furnace and return with Don to the dorm and the rest of the boys on this, my very first real Christmas night.

January 1939, found us still enjoying our Saturday afternoon movies. We were all boys who had known cold, so the short walk to town didn't hinder us any. One Saturday afternoon E.C., Mose, Don and I stopped at the drug store in town to look around and kill some time before heading back for supper. Walking up to the counter, I asked the salesclerk for a pack of Wings. Giving him the fifteen cents they cost, I casually strolled outside as I opened the pack. The boys followed me, dumbfounded.

"Are you crazy?" E.C. gasped, "Smoking? At 10 years old. Pop Hurley will beat you within an inch of your life."

Striking what I thought was a very grownup pose, I answered, "That's only if he catches me or someone tells on me." I knew they never would and I told them so.

"You're right," they replied in unison, "but he always finds out." Not sure what had possessed me to buy them, I offered both of them one.

"Nah," Mose answered, "It's not worth getting a whipping for and I don't know why you want to smoke anyway." E.C. and Don agreed with Mose.

"Well, I think its pretty neat," I told them, as I couldn't think of any other reason. Walking back to the school, they reminded me to hide them until we reached the dorm. Once inside my room, I hid them under my mattress, sure they were safe there.

Time passed with the routine of the week never changing. Rise up with the bell, fire the furnace, breakfast, chapel, check the furnace, school, check the furnace, free time, supper, free time, fire the furnace and sleep. There was a certain comfort in knowing what to expect each day, but boys will be boys and there were occasional fights that broke out. Whether from pent up energy, boredom with the routine, personality clashes or just someone choosing to bully someone, no one attempted to explain it. Fights were just a part of a lot of boys living together, I guess.

Lee was eight that spring and Jimmy had taken a real dislike to him for reasons no one could explain. Much bigger than Lee and older, he liked to bully him around. Pretty much a scrapper himself, Lee didn't like to come to me to defend him. He preferred to handle situations on his own even at such a young age. Unable to keep this from me though, I soon discovered the size and age of Jimmy, and, although I never believed on ganging up on one person, this was different. He was even bigger than I was. Explaining to Lee that this was a special situation and the only way to deal with bullies was with a dose of their own medicine. I came up with a plan.

Waiting on the second step of the stairs for Jimmy to come by, I told Lee, "You go low and I'll go high. We'll teach him to pick on you." Just as Jimmy came around the corner, he spotted Lee's red hair and grabbed for him. I flew off the step, grabbing him around the neck. Lee had sprung at him at exactly the same time and was latched onto his knees. We all hit the floor with a thud. Pounding his face with my fist and with Lee holding on like a tiger, he couldn't get away from us. Aunt Sis had, of course, heard the commotion and came running. Breaking up the fight, she summoned Dean Sublett. Since the rule concerning fighting was if no adult saw the fight start, all participants got the paddle. But, that paddling was quickly forgotten by Lee and I and well worth it we decided. We knew Jimmy had learned not to mess with the Lambert boys and he never did again.

The days were getting warmer and my job was easing up. The furnace didn't need fired quite as often during the day and soon would be shut down completely. With a little more free time, since Pop wouldn't give me a new job until then, I would sneak into the outhouse for an occasional smoke.

"Oh, God, I'm dead now," I thought when I stepped out of there and almost stepped on Pop.

"You been smoking, Paul?" he asked accusingly.

Knowing better than to lie to him, I answered honestly, "Yes, sir, I guess I have."

"You know I don't allow smoking, don't you?" he asked,

although I knew he didn't expect an answer. He pulled his paddle from behind him and proceeded with my paddling. It was my first from him and one I wouldn't soon forget. Unfortunately, it didn't stop me from smoking.

My buddies gave me quite a razzing over Pop catching me smoking.

"We tried to warn you," E.C. reminded me, "Not much gets past Pop." Having learned that lesson the hard way, all I could do was agree with them. Laughing, we made our way up the mountainside. It was a nice, spring afternoon and we were anxious to get out of school and explore. We checked on our walnut and hickory nut trees to be sure they had survived the winter, since these were a source of income for us. They had survived and we ventured on to be sure the huckleberries, raspberries and blackberries were greening up. Everywhere we looked, things were springing back to life and we felt a renewed energy ourselves. Spring had arrived in the mountains and it felt good.

Easter Sunday dawned bright and sunny. I was sure it was going to warm up, as there wasn't a cloud in the sky as I walked to the furnace room. I fired up the furnace to take the morning chill off the building, knowing Pop would allow me to leave it until evening. I always wore the best clothes I had for Sunday morning church, but I made a special effort this morning. Easter was special, even though the celebration wasn't quite like Christmas; everyone had looked forward to its arrival. I finished with the furnace and walked slowly to breakfast, enjoying the sun and the buds popping out on the trees. For a brief moment, I thought of Aunt Annie and Uncle Luther. I remembered how much they loved spring and the rebirth it promised.

Sitting down with my friends for breakfast, I hadn't noticed what I thought was the smell of bacon frying until that moment. My mind had been everywhere else, I guess, and I wondered if it was my imagination.

"Is that bacon I smell?" I asked everyone, hopefully.

"Sure is," Tommy answered. He was another friend at our table.

"We get bacon and fried eggs for Easter breakfast," Mose added.

"Just one time a year," E.C. continued, "and this is it." As if on cue, the girls began serving, delivering bacon, eggs, and toast to each of us. After countless bowls of oatmeal, that one egg tasted better than anything else I could imagine. We may not have had the chocolate bunnies or baskets we had seen in town, but I don't think there was a kid in the dining room who would have switched their egg for one at that moment.

May arrived and my furnace job was over until cold weather returned. The last couple of months had been pretty easy, as the days had warmed. Aunt Sis had been talking about getting the garden started, so I expected to be hoeing and planting soon. We were finishing the school year and normally had free time after school, but not now.

"Gardens need planted as soon as it's warm enough," Pop explained. "It can't wait, if we want to have vegetables this summer." Most all of us knew about planting and gardening from our past, so we didn't complain. We had learned already that "you had to make hay while the sun shines" was a true statement. Aunt Sis had already planted a few things that didn't mind the cool temperatures, but she needed us to do the bulk of it now that it had warmed up. Dean Sublett had taken the older boys to the fields to plant the corn we grew to feed the dairy cows. They had been working on that after school and on Saturdays for a few weeks now. I wasn't surprised when Pop told me I'd be working for Aunt Sis in the garden. We hoed and planted, hoed and planted, and hoed and planted some more. I began to feel as if she was planting for the entire town, not just for us. It felt good to be out in the sun with the other boys, though, instead of down in the cement, furnace pit alone.

School was out for the year and summer had officially arrived. The fields and gardens were planted, but we were kept busy with hoeing weeds, mowing grass, making repairs, painting, and anything else Pop or Dean Sublett felt needed done around the grounds. We boys did all the outside work. The girls had plenty to do inside, with the cooking, cleaning, canning, and laundry. We still had plenty of time to play, swim, earn our own money, see movies, and just enjoy being boys of summer.

After breakfast one July Saturday, Pop stopped me and asked me to find Lee and meet him in his office. As I looked around for Lee, I tried to figure out what Pop needed us for that morning. If he had caught me doing something wrong, he would have handled that already. He didn't postpone punishment, but handed it out on the spot. Locating Lee, we quickly made our way to the office, not wanting to keep Pop waiting for long and not sure what to expect.

One step inside his office and I knew why we were summoned. Sitting by his desk was our Mom with a red-haired lady I suspected was Doug's wife. Madeline had written earlier in the month and told us that he had gotten married. We had no idea Mom was coming for a visit, though, and if Madeline had known, she hadn't told us. Neither of us had seen Mom for quite some time, although we had received a couple letters from her since we had been at the school. I didn't know how to react, since I wasn't sure why she was here. Understanding our hesitation without saying, Pop took over.

"Your Mom is here to take you boys into town for a visit," he explained. "You're free to go. We'll take care of your chores today."

"Thank you, Pop," we both answered as we walked out together without any show of affection among us. Mom never offered either of us a hug or a kiss and we didn't either. To me, they were just some ladies who had come to visit Lee and me. I didn't feel much one way or the other and I don't believe Lee did either.

Reaching the car they had come in, Mom introduced us to Mamie, the red-haired lady. She had brought Mom to visit us, leaving Doug at home working. I wished he had been with them, since I hadn't seen him since our shanty boat summer. Parking near the theater, we walked around talking until lunch. Mamie was a skinny, shy sister-in-law without much to say to Lee or me. She really didn't know us and we had been out of contact with Doug for quite some time, so he couldn't have told her much. We ate lunch, went to a movie and stopped at the clothing store in town. They bought Lee and me a shirt and a pair of pants apiece before we headed back to the school. Mamie asked Lee and me to pose with Mom in front of the school. Doug had asked her to take a picture, before she left, so he could see we were all right, she told us. With a peck on the cheek for each of us, they were quickly on their way home. Feeling neither sadness nor loss at their leaving, Lee and I carried our new clothes to the dorm and met the other boys for supper. This was all the family we knew.

Lee, Mom, Paul 1939   *Lee, Mamie, Paul 1939*

Dean Sublett and Pop kept a pretty tight rein of us for the most part, but it was impossible to watch that many children all the time. We managed to get into a little mischief from time to time that summer, as all boys do when given the opportunity. Nothing real bad, no destruction or harm to others, but on our way back from working at the dairy farm, we would often swipe a few apples from the farm next door. Fortunately, for us, his trees were near the road and on a good day, we could get not only a few to eat, but enough to sell in town for a little pocket change. We routinely listened for a truck straining to climb the mountain road beside the school. If free from chores, we would run to catch it and see what it was hauling. Watermelons were the best prize, because invariably some would roll off the truck as it climbed higher and higher. Nothing tasted better than ill-gotten watermelon to a bunch of ragamuffin boys. If Pop knew, he never let on, and we didn't believe he did. He would have made us pay for them. I continued smoking and consequently was caught and paddled more times, than I care to remember.

The days rolled on and soon school was again in session. The weather turned cold and I was back in the furnace. Another birthday passed, then the wonderful Christmas celebration and before I knew it, 1940 was here. Franie had written that she now had two boys and had moved to Huntington, West Virginia. Loretta had gotten divorced and was living in Charleston, she added. Lee and I received letters from Madeline more often than from anyone, but never any from our brothers and rarely from Mom. Nothing much changed for us as we continued to live in the safety and security of the school.

I was eleven years old for most of 1940, as my birthday was late in the year. Life for me was routine, but satisfying and Lee and I had both developed a strong nucleus of friends. We never forgot that we were brothers, but he had his buddies and I had mine. Mose, Don, E.C. and I could usually be found together whenever we had any free time away from school and chores. I learned that sometimes, no change in what you expect is a good thing.

A couple of months into the new school year, I woke up with a big lump under each ear. I had been sick before with earaches, but I knew this was different. E.C. took one look at me and went to get Aunt Sis despite my telling him I was ok. She quickly diagnosed the mumps on both sides.

"How do you feel, Paul," she asked.

"I'm ok," I replied, "My neck just feels funny." Checking to be sure that I didn't have a fever, she told me I could go on to my job and school if I felt like I wanted to.

"You're not contagious," she said. "Just don't be running and jumping around. We don't want them to go down on you. You'll really be sick then," she advised me as she left my room. Getting dressed, E.C. asked me if I was sure, I felt ok.

"Yea, I'm ok," I answered him. "Probably get teased though with these jaws."

He reassured me, laughing, "Mumps seem to go through the school, so before it's over, you'll probably have company." I finished dressing and we headed out for the day.

I fired the furnace, being sure to get a good fire going and went on to breakfast, chapel and school. After supper, I checked the furnace and added plenty of coal, before heading to bed. I was a little more tired than usual, but figured that was to be expected. The mumps were a type of illness, I supposed, so maybe this was normal. The next day passed a little slower, as I began to not feel so good. By Thursday, I was sick at my stomach and my private parts were swollen enough to scare me. Not sure what was wrong with me, I asked E.C. to get Aunt Sis. Hating to admit being sick, I was attempting to get dressed when she arrived.

"Oh, no you don't," she exclaimed. "You get right back in that bed and let me look at you."

When I didn't object, E.C. grew concerned, "What's wrong with him?" he asked Aunt Sis.

"Well, I suspect the mumps have gone down on him. You weren't running or jumping were you, Paul?"

"No, ma'am," I answered, "I did just what you told me."

Waving E.C. toward the door, Aunt Sis told him, "You'd better get Pop for me. Tell him Paul is pretty sick."

I drifted in and out of sleep, as Aunt Sis waited with me for Pop to arrive. In no time, he was there and with one look at me, he told Aunt Sis to keep me in bed. "I'll call the doctor to be sure, but I think that's all we can do for him," he added. As they left my room, I heard Don tell Pop that he would take care of the

JUDY LAMBERT

furnace for me. What a friend, I thought, as I fell asleep as the nausea overtook me again. Sometime later, Aunt Sis woke me and fed me some soup.

"The doctor doesn't feel he needs to see you," she said. "But you have to stay in bed for a few days."

"I don't know how this happened", I told her, and "I did what you said."

"The doctor believes it was caused by shoveling the coal," she explained, "I feel terrible, but I didn't think about that being so strenuous."

"It's not your fault, Aunt Sis," I told her. I sure didn't want her to feel bad. I felt bad enough for both of us. By Sunday evening, I was feeling better and although Aunt Sis let me go to school on Monday, Pop wouldn't let me go back to the furnace until Thursday. I never thought I would look forward to my job, but it sure beat feeling that bad.

It took a little while to get back up to par, but soon my buddies and I were out gathering our walnuts and hickory nuts. They provided a tidy, little sum of money for us and our lady customers in town were loyal to us and counted on our deliveries. The days grew colder and we knew it wouldn't be long before Christmas would be here. This was the most special time of the year for us and we all looked forward to it.

The anticipation and all the extra activity leading up to the big day was as much a part of Christmas, as the day itself. For some of the kids, it was the Christmas tree all lit up, for others, the Christmas plays, and yet for a lot of the kids, it was the special Christmas dinner with cookies. For me, it was the brown, paper bag filled with an orange, apple, and hard tack candy that Pop always handed to me on Christmas day. Oh, sure, everyone appreciated the gifts we received, whatever they were, but they were seldom mentioned when we reminisced later on. It was the other things that really stuck with us.

The new year brought no changes to our life at the school. Chores continued needing done and school had to be attended. We still ate oatmeal every morning and pinto beans, potatoes, and cornbread every evening. Every morning started with chapel, which most of us had come to depend on for reassurance. Aunt Sis was still our housemother and Dean Sublett remained Pop's right hand man. Lee and I still got occasional letters from Franie and Madeline, as they tried to keep in touch with us as best they could. Letters from Loretta had stopped coming and neither Franie nor Madeline had mentioned where she was currently. Maybe she hadn't stayed in touch with them either, I supposed. The rare letter from Mom had stopped, also.

By the spring of 1941, I had asked Pop and been given permission to buy a paper route from one of the older boys at the school who wanted to sell his route. Even though the five dollars he asked for it took most of the money I had, I figured it would be worth it. He always seemed to have plenty of money and I was used to getting up early.

"You got to get the papers to the men before they leave for work," Joe told me as he took my money. "They don't like missing their paper and will get it from someone else if you're late." Giving me his list of addresses and explaining where to pick up the papers, I assured him I would do a good job. The papers had to be delivered before breakfast, but not until I had fired the furnace. Being allowed to have an outside job was a privilege, but it didn't relieve me of my responsibilities at the school. I could continue as long as it didn't interfere with my chores or school. Some mornings had me starting out in the dark, but at a penny a paper and three cents for Sundays, I knew it wouldn't be long before I could buy myself a bicycle. I was delivering fifty papers a day, which added up to four dollars and a half each week and I knew I'd have the used bicycle I had been eyeing in no time. Ten dollars was money well spent, I decided, as I paid the boy his asking price after only three short weeks. The bicycle allowed me to deliver much faster and make it back to the school in time for breakfast. It wouldn't be long and the furnace would be shut down for the warm months. The route would be easier at that point and I would be familiar with it before it turned cold again. I appreciated Pop allowing me to do this and I made sure that I did the best job possible and that no one had reason to complain to Pop. I wanted him to be proud of me.

Pop was determined to keep the girls separated from the boys. It was a rule he was adamant about and had made clear from the beginning. A row of trees on both sides of the path separated our dorm from theirs. We were never allowed past the tree line, nor were they. Although we saw them in the dining room, chapel and at school, we weren't allowed to talk to them alone, one on one. That was why we weren't allowed to go to the movies or into Grundy on the same day. It goes without saying, that physical contact was strictly forbidden. I suppose, with that many children of both sexes, there had to be a lot of supervision. I didn't mind the rule in the beginning, as I was perfectly content to hang out with my buddies. Approaching thirteen, however, my viewpoint took a dramatic turn. Try as he might, even Pop couldn't stop nature from taking her natural course.

Annie was the prettiest girl in my school, or so I thought. She had long, dark hair and green eyes, which sparkled when she smiled at me. I was smitten! When she slipped me a school picture, I treasured it and promised to keep it near my heart forever. She was always on my mind and every glimpse of her set my heart racing. Mose, being a little older than me, understood how I felt and didn't tease me.

We were standing on the bridge beside the school, throwing rocks in the river one afternoon, late in the spring. Mose asked me which girl it was that I had such a crush on.

"Annie," I replied, "She's really pretty." Mose stood thinking, trying to put a face to the name, I guess. "I've got her picture, if you want to see," I offered.

"Sure do," Mose answered. Reaching into my shirt pocket where I always kept it, I pulled it out. Just as I started to hand it to Mose, the wind picked up and blew it out of my hand. I watched, horrified, as the wind stopped and Annie's picture floated towards the water. "No, don't," I heard Mose yell as I jumped, fully dressed, into the river. Swimming like mad, I reached her picture and snatched it out of the water. Now, I realized how icy cold the river was and quickly made for the

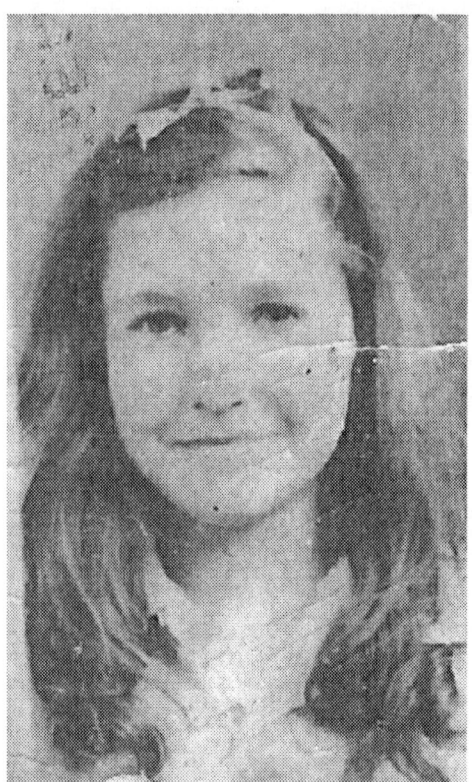

bank. Mose was waiting for me on the bank, reached down, and pulled me out. He just shook his head, as he muttered, "Must be true love to do a fool thing like that." I just smiled as we headed for the dorm to get out of my wet clothes. I still had Annie's picture and that was all that mattered.

My first girlfriend

I wasn't anxious for the school year to end. Seeing Annie every day was something I looked forward to and made going to school effortless. In spite of my wishes, however, it did end. Summer arrived with the outside chores and additional projects Dean Sublett or Pop had for us and the additional free time to explore and have fun. I saw Annie briefly at meals and chapel and my love for her died of neglect, I suppose.

Almost two years to the day from when Mom had first visited us, she arrived again. This time she had come alone, and after being summoned to Pop's office to greet her, we walked into town to spend the day together. Not really having much memory of her as our Mom, it felt strange being with her. We appreciated a visit from anyone, but I felt a little guilty that I didn't know how to be with her. While we were eating lunch, she told us that a doctor and his wife had requested permission to adopt us. She informed us that she had refused when Pop had contacted her. Oddly enough, I was disappointed she had refused, but happy to know that someone wanted me. I couldn't understand her refusing as that would have provided Lee and I with a real home life. She couldn't explain, except to tell us we were hers and she wasn't giving us away. This made no sense to me, considering where and how we were living. She had no intention of taking us with her that was apparent. Questioning her any further proved futile and we made our way to the movies to pass the time. Mom didn't seem to know how to act with us any more than we did her. She offered us no updates on the family and not knowing if she had any contact with our brothers or sisters, we didn't ask anything. Leaving the theater, we walked her to the bus stop and waited for her bus to arrive. With a quick goodbye, Lee and I walked back to the school discussing what we had been told, not sure when we would see her again.

No one loved the movies any more than Lee, and he would sneak off to them whenever he got a chance. Since I had started my paper route and had a steady income, I shared that with Lee. He was still my little brother and I looked out for him. Giving him twenty-five cents a week allowance allowed him a couple movies a week. At only nine cents each for the movie, he had money left over for a moon pie or oatmeal pie he loved. Having turned ten in April, he had much less supervision than when he was younger and always took care of his chores before heading off. Everyone knew how he felt about the movies and Pop would routinely catch and paddle him. He didn't seem to mind, though, and would be right back to the movies, as soon as he thought the coast was clear.

I, on the other hand, continued to think I could get by with smoking and would get caught and paddled about as often as Lee did for sneaking out to the movies. Unfortunately, it didn't stop me, either. Now that girls were something of interest to me, they became another reason for getting paddled. Pop had an eagle eye for spotting me trying to talk to them, sneak them apples I had stolen or just trying to get their attention. I couldn't seem to resist the allure of the fair sex.

As I had anticipated, my paper route was much easier that summer. I was always up before the bell and with not having to fire the furnace; I would be dressed and gone on my bicycle before E.C. would be awake. Our newspapers came in from Ashland, Kentucky, as Grundy wasn't large enough to have its own newspaper. We were always a day behind on the news, but everyone was used to that and didn't seem to mind. I was enjoying the extra money and it was better to have a regular job than scratch for odd jobs all summer long.

A decent, generous man, Pop was a good member of the community of Grundy as well as head of the school. When the town folks needed to build a church, he didn't hesitate to offer our help. Most of the week was spent on our regular chores and the things the school needed done, but come Saturday morning, we would be at the church site in town, as soon as we finished breakfast. Depending on the age of each boy, we would be sawing, hammering or some type of carpentry work, carrying mortar for the brick layers, helping lay brick, working on the roof or whatever needed done according to our ability. Whatever skill was needed, we seemed to have someone who could fill the bill and get it done.

Being older, I was put to work measuring and sawing timber, while Lee was carrying mortar for the brick layers. These men were hard working, country folks donating their time and effort for the good of the church.

Lee, always cheerful whatever he was doing, greeted them with a hardy, "How ya doin?" as he delivered his bucket.

"I'm busier than a man with two women," one of them replied as the rest just chuckled and nodded agreement. Being only ten years old, I had no idea what that meant. Later on when he got a chance to question me, I told him not to worry about it, he'd understand some day. I didn't tell him, but I wasn't even sure what they meant either, but figured it was an adult thing somehow. Sending him back to work, I could see him pondering it in his mind.

The summer flew by and before we knew it, the church was completed. We all felt good about our work. We hadn't forgotten the generosity the town showed us each Christmas and knew it was a privilege to do something for them in return. Soon school was back in session. The daily routine returned and everyone fell back in step easily.

In October, I became a teenager and Pop made me a part of the singing group. The school was private and supported by

Pop and Mom Hurley and whatever donations they could acquire. Pop actively pursued support, knowing he couldn't continue the school without help and refusing to accept government intervention. He had formed a group of teenage boys to sing gospel songs and travel with him to speaking engagements he arranged. I was excited to be included, even though I didn't know for how long. We all knew he rotated the boys regularly to be fair and to give everyone who wanted a chance to take part. I decided to make the most of my opportunity and looked forward to the occasional excursions around the state.

November was a good time to ask for support according to Pop. The holiday season was approaching and people became more aware of those less fortunate it seemed. Packed into Pop's 1940's, black Chrysler, the eight of us traveled to Hurley for my first excursion outside of Grundy and the school. Although I loved to sing and had been singing my whole life, it was a little scary to be in front of so many people I didn't know. I was grateful that most of the other boys had done this before and helped me feel comfortable. After a couple songs, Pop took the podium and by the time he finished speaking, he had convinced me to give him every dime I had. I was inspired and knew he had touched his audience. The minister took up a collection from the audience and it appeared to me to be generous. We, of course, would never know, as that was Pop's private business, and we never questioned him. We sang another song in closing and drove back to the school, feeling good about what we had helped accomplish.

December 7, 1941 dawned sunny and clear and no one suspected what the day would bring, as we gathered for breakfast, church and lunch. Having the rest of the day to ourselves, we were hanging around the dorm, when word began spreading around the school that our country had been attacked. We were all aware of a great war being waged in Europe from the newsreels we saw at the movies, but no one expected us to be attacked. We gathered around every available radio for the latest news. The Japanese had attacked Pearl Harbor, Hawaii that morning. It was a surprise attack and many ships and men had been lost, according to the radio broadcast. President Roosevelt was preparing to make an announcement, they reported and all the grownups feared the news. Everything came to a standstill at the school, while we huddled around whatever radio we were close to. "I have declared the United States to be at war with the Japanese "came the President's voice over the radio. He continued speaking, but most of us didn't hear much more. We were stunned and not sure what that would mean to any of us. Were we going to be attacked, too, the younger kids wondered? Many of us had older brothers, who, although we may not have seen them for a while, they were still our brothers. They might have to go to war if it lasted very long. I couldn't help but think of Johnny, Doug and Walt, even though I didn't know where they were or what they were doing.

Reluctantly, as no one wanted to leave the radios, we walked over to the dining hall for our Sunday sandwiches. All desire to eat had quickly left us after hearing the news of war. The entire place was a buzz. The adults were all gathered together looking more distressed than I had ever seen them. Pop stood up, knowing that many of the younger children were scared. He reassured all of us, explaining Hawaii was a far ways off and he was confident we were not in any danger. He said the prayer himself, asking God's hand on our soldiers and sailors, as well as our country and our President. We all joined him in that prayer. Mose, E.C., Don, and I couldn't stop talking about the news.

"Do you think any of the older boys will have to go?" Don asked Mose. Being fifteen at the time, we knew he was too young, but some of his other friends were older.

"I don't think so," he said, "most of the older boys leave as soon as they finish school. The ones still here aren't old enough."

"What about L.C.?" E.C. enquired, "He's old enough, isn't he?"

L.C. Lambert, no relation to Lee and me, was the oldest boy at the school. A nice guy, who the girls considered rather good-looking, was the "big man on campus." Not only big in size, he was a leader and someone all of us boys looked up to. I guess, next to Dean Sublett, Pop depended on L.C. to help him out whenever he needed him. He drove the singing group whenever Pop chose to take a bigger group than could fit into one car and the dump truck when we needed sand. We couldn't imagine the place without him and we waited anxiously to hear what would happen to him, knowing he was old enough to be called to war.

Picking up the papers early that December 8, I knew everyone would be anxious to receive it. "PEARL HARBOR ATTACKED! WAR DECLARED!" Read the headlines, as I loaded my bicycle.

"You're a little late with that news, boy," an old gentleman standing nearby reminded me.

"Yes, I know, sir." I replied, "But I deliver them when I get them. Still a lot to read looks like." Peddling off, I saw some of my customers standing outside waiting for my arrival. Grabbing the paper, they rushed back inside, anxious looks on many faces. I could have sold as many papers as I could carry that day.

School that day was filled with Pearl Harbor, the President, and war. Anyone who wasn't sure where Pearl Harbor was or what declaring war meant, knew by the end of the day. Without trying to scare anyone, every teacher made sure that we were aware of the historical significance of what had happened. As the President had said, "This is a day that will live in infamy." I wasn't quite sure what that meant when I heard it the first time, but by the end of the day, I understood. A patriotic spirit prevailed throughout the school and we couldn't wait until Saturday to get to the movies. We knew the newsreels would be full of Pearl Harbor news.

Sure enough, the newsreel that Saturday was longer than normal. We all sit in stunned silence as we saw the bombs dropping on the ships and saw the President make his speech. It was quite an experience for us and one we would remember for a long time. I don't think any of us remembered the movie we saw afterward. All we talked about going back to the school was the newsreel and the patriotic symbols all over Grundy's two blocks. Flags and red, white and blue bunting were displayed everywhere you looked.

The war had no direct impact on us, and except for the news broadcasts we heard on the radio and the newsreels we saw at the movies, life continued on relatively uneventful. We were aware of all the flags flying to show support for the war effort and the boys from Grundy who had joined up. Everywhere we went, we saw symbols of our national pride. Our singing group had made quite a few appearances that December and Pop appeared satisfied as we arrived home from our latest, Sunday, afternoon trip.

"We may have to make a few trips after the New Year," he explained to us, "but for now, it's time we prepared for Christmas." None of us was disappointed with that. "This Saturday we'll cut the tree," he said. "You boys get on to supper now."

The Christmas preparations took on special meaning that year with the country at war. Although the war was more of a grown-ups concern, we knew that a lot of families would be without their sons and husbands this year. Grateful that we had each other and wasn't alone, we seemed to draw closer without really understanding why. Maybe we knew what being scared and alone felt like and we could relate to them. I don't know why, but from decorating the tree to the last Christmas cookie eaten, Christmas of 1941 was extra special for all of us.

The New Year brought an added responsibility to me. Pop was very particular about everyone's appearance and insisted on regular showers, clean clothes, haircuts and shaves as needed. Dean Sublett observed me cutting Lee's hair, as I had always done for him.

"You do that pretty good, boy." he commented to me. "Think you could do a few for me?" he asked.

"Sure, Dean, if you want me to and they don't mind." I answered.

Turning, he asked, "Well, boys, how about it?" Quickly they began lining up in response. "Well, Paul, I guess that's our answer." Dean stated. From then on, I became the school barber. You could find me most Saturday mornings from then on, cutting head after head of boy's hair. It wasn't anything fancy, just short and neat for the older boys and a burr for the younger ones. That helped keep the spread of lice down which was always a problem with that many children roomed together.

The girls did all of the laundry for the school, which was then sorted and placed in a large closet in the dorm. Stacks of pants, shirts, underwear, socks and t-shirts of various sizes were arranged on shelves to be selected by each boy for the day. Some days everything fit well and some days not so well. As I had gotten older, I became more particular about my clothing. When I was fortunate enough to choose something that fit well, I accepted Aunt Sis's rule, and kept it knowing I would have to take care of it myself. I taught myself to replace buttons, turn up a hem and stitch it, make simple repairs and how to iron. It was well worth it to me, though. To be able to be comfortable in my clothes and proud of my appearance meant a lot.

Miss Spring had continued to be special to me. I'm not sure why she took such an interest in me, but she was always aware of how and what I was doing. I knew I could go to her at anytime for help with schoolwork or any other concern I might have. All the kids liked her and she made it apparent that she loved teaching and the children she taught.

It was the evening of Good Friday when someone knocked on my dorm room door. I was speechless when I opened it to find Miss Spring standing there. It was more than a little unusual for a teacher to come to you for anything and I wasn't sure what to do or how to act.

"I just wanted to give this to you," she stated, handing me a rectangular box. "This seemed the perfect time." She stood in the doorway without making any motion to enter.

"You want to come in?" I asked, not sure if I should even ask that.

"Oh, no," she replied, "But I would like for you to open the box before I leave. It's something I want you to have." Opening it quickly, I was thrilled to see a black Bible in the box.

"Thank you, Miss Spring," I stammered, "I don't have a Bible."

With a quiet smile, she replied, "I know, but you should." I wanted to hug her, but didn't, not sure it would be a proper thing to do. I walked her downstairs thanking her repeatedly. Offering to walk her back to her room, she politely refused.

"I'll be quite alright," she said as she waved goodbye. Returning to my dorm room and my new Bible, I realized she had signed and dated it for me. I intended to keep it forever, a gift from my favorite teacher of all time.

Spring in the mountains is a glorious time. With all the plants and trees coming back to life, the entire area becomes shades of greens, pinks, purples and whites. The sights, the smells of new blossoms and the sounds of the little animals scurrying about can't help but make you feel good all over, inside and out. The spring sun and cloudless days tends to give everyone "spring fever." However, the warmer weather meant the gardens and fields had to be planted, grass had to be mowed, and we didn't have time to dwaddle. Shortly the end of another year of school would be upon us. The war had continued and letters from family were even more infrequent than before. Lee and I had not received any news about our brothers and we tried not to think about where they might be or if they were safe.

Pop put us to work that summer making cement blocks to construct a work shed for the schools outside equipment. Making blocks wasn't difficult, only time consuming. The blocks required sand, water, and cement, which we mixed and poured into forms to create blocks. We had a ready supply of sand down at the riverbank. The river ran right past the school. Just a little ways down, it turned slightly and made a nice, sandy beach area. L.C. normally drove the dump truck, but having already graduated, he had left right after Christmas to join the war effort. James would drive us now. A crew of us jumped into the back with shovels in hand and James made his way to the river. Piling out of the back, we began shoveling the sand in to fill the truck. This was the hardest part of the job, but the reward of riding back on top of the sand was worth it. That was one of our most favorite things to do. Besides, we only had to do it once a day. One load would make all the blocks we could manage to make in a day.

It was about our third trip to the sand, I suppose, when things didn't go quite as planned. The bank was steep where James approached the sand. A certain angle was required to maneuver that big truck to where it needed to be to be filled. There were about ten boys of various sizes, including Lee and myself, in the back of the truck as he drove along. We grew concerned when it became apparent that James had gotten the right wheels too high on the bank.

"JUMP!" someone yelled and suddenly ten boys were in the air at one time. The truck tilted left, with a thunderous noise rolled over on its side, and then, as suddenly, rolled again, righting itself. Poor James was froze to the steering wheel as it had went over repeatedly. Picking myself up, I looked around frantically for Lee, who I couldn't find. Screaming his name, I was terrified the truck had crushed him.

"Paul, Paul," he yelled from somewhere, "I'm up here." Turning around, I looked up and waving from a tree was Lee, hanging onto a branch. As I helped him down, he explained that he was on the high side of the truck and the tree was just there for him as he leaped. We gathered around the truck, counting each other to be sure we were all there. We quickly realized that it was only the grace of God that we had all survived and none of us, including James, had a scratch.

We eventually got the truck filled and returned to the school. Pop was concerned as to what had taken so long, questioning if we decided to take a swim.

"No, sir," James hesitantly explained. "I turned the truck over." Before he could say another word, Pop was instantly questioning whether anyone was hurt in any way. We all began at one time telling him what had happened. He breathed a sigh of relief when it was apparent that we all thought it was a great adventure. James was very apologetic, but Pop quickly put a stop to that.

"Accidents can happen to anyone," he said. "Did you learn anything?"

"Oh, yes sir," James replied. "I surely did." Many more trips were made that summer, but James had gotten the scare of his young life and had learned the lesson extremely well. There were no more close calls and the work shed got built to everyone's satisfaction, especially Pop's.

E.C., Don, Mose and I continued attending the Saturday

movies. We went as much for the newsreels, to keep abreast of the war, as for the movie. We continued to enjoy swimming in the river, visiting our caves in the mountain and generally hanging out together. I still accompanied Pop on occasional outing to the various churches to solicit support for the school. I had not been replaced in the singing group, so I didn't question it. I was enjoying the trips tremendously, as much for the change in the daily routine as the traveling.

E.C. and Mose, My Buddies

The Virginia trees are a stunning mixture of oranges, greens, yellows, reds and purples as they prepare for the winter. Fall was upon us and an extremely busy time at the school, especially for us older boys. Immediately after school, Mose, Don, E.C., and I would head down the road to the dairy farm where we met up with the other boys. Grabbing our two-foot long, corn knives, we headed to the fields. Ready for harvest, the corn now had to be cut down, the ears removed and the stalks formed into shocks before the snow began falling. Shucking the ears as we moved down the rows, we filled bushel basket after bushel basket. We worked a few hours after school each day and all day Saturdays until every ear was in the corncrib. Most of it would be used to feed the cows, but some would be taken out for the chickens and a small portion would be ground into cornmeal for the school. Once the corn was in, we knew it wouldn't be long until winter would be upon us.

We all looked forward to the last Thursday in November. Thanksgiving was the beginning of a special time at the school. Rushing back to the dorm after getting the furnace going good, I got a shower and a shave before breakfast. Now fourteen, I had to shave every day, as Pop had no tolerance for a face that needed shaving. Knowing the day would be filled with good things, I sure didn't want to give Pop any reason to be upset with me. My buddies and I walked down to the auditorium for chapel after breakfast. We knew from past experience that our service today would be a bit longer as Pop made sure we appreciated all our blessings and this day of Thanksgiving. Although, I tried very hard to pay attention, I must admit, my mind drifted over to the kitchen a time or two.

We wandered back to the dorm, knowing we had a few hours to kill before the big meal. With no school or no chores to do, we hardly knew what to do with ourselves. Not paying any attention to the coolness of the morning, since it wasn't really that cold, we stayed outside just hanging around talking about girls as we normally did. Being so segregated from them made them that much more enticing, if that's possible for teenage boys. Aunt Sis stepped outside to let us know it was time to eat. She barely got the words out of her mouth and we were gone in a flash, knowing what was in store for us.

"There's nothing that smells as good as Thanksgiving," I said to E.C. as we seated ourselves.

"Yep," he answered, "I think it's my favorite holiday." Before we could say anymore, Pop stood and asked Dean Sublett to say the blessing. Everyone stood, as he prayed, giving thanks for all we had and remembering those serving our country in the war. Shortly after we sat, the girls began serving. What a feast they presented to us. Turkey, gravy, dressing, mashed potatoes, greens, sweet potatoes, corn and rolls, as much as we wanted too. But we weren't stupid either. We knew there were pumpkin pies and apple pies still waiting for us. We made sure to save some room for them. Most of the kids preferred pumpkin, but our table all chose apple. By the end of that wonderful meal, we all agreed we couldn't eat another bite for a week.

Of course, we were boys and by supper, we were ready to eat again. As we did on Sundays, this day we also had sandwiches, but after the Thanksgiving dinner the girls had prepared for us, there was not a boy in the place who would have complained. Someone would have probably beaten them to a pulp if they had tried to anyway. I don't think any of us were hungry; it was just what we did at that time of day. We took our time that evening, talking, joking, laughing, and sneaking glances and winks at the girls when we thought no one was looking.

The Christmas season was another wonderful celebration,

and before long, another year had arrived. My days were pretty full with having to shave every day, taking care of my own clothes, running my paper route, taking care of the furnace, school, cutting hair and the singing group. I still had time with my friends and to keep an eye on Lee and I was content. It was what I knew and I was comfortable with it. I still managed to get caught smoking or flirting with the girls and suffered the consequences. I was sure that would be my fate for some time to come since I simply couldn't resist either.

Movies were the only entertainment available to us in Grundy, but my buddies and I didn't mind. We continued to attend every other week and enjoyed the escape to another world and time that the movies provided. There was a soda shop in town, but without a girl to take with us, it didn't seem to hold much charm. Pop kept such a close eye on them, we didn't have a prayer of getting close to them. There were a few girls from Grundy at the movies occasionally and Pop had never forbidden us from dating them. But, not having attended school with them made it difficult to get acquainted. We didn't have enough experience with girls to be suave and debonair like Errol Flynn or the other leading men we saw in the movies.They were never too eager to approach us either. I suppose Pop was well aware of that fact and knew he had no cause for concern.

Spring passed quickly that year. Shortly after school was out for the year, Lee and I got the surprise of our young lives. Having been requested to locate Lee and bring him to Pop's office with me, we expected that someone had come for a visit. In the past, that had been the only reason Pop had requested us both at the same time. We knocked on his door, expectantly, prepared to greet Mom or maybe one of our sisters.

"Sit down boys," Pop said, "I've got some news for you," he

continued as he reached for a letter. My heart raced, as I wasn't sure what news that might be. Pop seemed so serious, I was afraid he had some kind of bad news, perhaps concerning our brothers with the war and all.

Hesitantly, I asked, "What kind of news, Pop?" Realizing we feared bad news, he quickly put us at ease.

"It's not anything bad," he said, "Just something a little different for you boys." As I breathed a sigh of relief, he proceeded to explain that our Mom wanted to come and take us back to Dayton, Ohio with her. "Just for a week's vacation," he promptly added, being sure we understood we would be returning to the school and not staying with her. "Do you want to go?" He asked, "It's up to you two." I glanced at Lee who was nodding his agreement.

"Sure, Pop," I answered, "We'd like to go. Never seen Ohio. Do you know when she's coming?" He explained that he would write her immediately giving his permission and would let us know as soon as he heard from her.

"She indicated that she would like to come as soon as possible, so I would expect her in a couple weeks," he stated. We left his office excited at the prospect of a real trip.

Eight days later, Mom arrived without any notice. Pop was use to kids leaving for a few days, off and on, during the summer. A lot of the kids had some family member who took them out of the school for a few days occasionally during the summer. He handled us leaving without any difficulty even though I was sure he would have appreciated some advance notice. Nevertheless, he didn't let on and wished us a good trip. We climbed into the back seat of the 1936, black Chevy and Mom introduced us to Walter. I didn't know if he was her husband or just a friend. She never said and since it really didn't matter to me, I didn't ask her. Finally, on the way, Lee and I settled down for the ride to Dayton, Ohio. The breeze was warm coming in the window and with the steady rhythm of the road, we were asleep before we got out of Virginia.

Startled out of my sleep by a loud clanging noise, I couldn't believe my eyes. Rubbing them to be sure I was seeing clearly, I looked again. Before me, as far as I could see, was flat land. I could even see the horizon.

"Is this Ohio?" I excitedly asked Mom.

"Yes, we're almost there," she answered. I was fascinated by so much flatland and I promised myself, in that moment, that I'd come back to this someday for good. "Walter has to fix the fan belt. That was the noise that woke you," she explained. "Then we'll be on our way again. Shouldn't take long." I didn't care how long it took. I was enthralled with what I was seeing for the first time ever and just stared out the window.

It was dark by the time we arrived at Mom's house in the city. We couldn't tell much about the neighborhood in the dark. We had slept off and on most of the way, but we had no problem going to sleep. Morning would come soon enough we decided.

We woke up early, anxious to see what the day had in store for us.

"Your sisters want to see you boys," Mom told us during breakfast. "We'll go see Franie when we finish breakfast." Walter drove us to Orchard Street where Franie lived with her husband, Jim, and two sons, Harold and Jimmy. She was excited to see us and how we had grown. We talked up a blue streak as she filled us in on everyone. Since the war, Johnny and Doug had joined the Army and were unharmed at the present time. Walt had been in the Merchant Marines, but had joined the Navy recently. Franie wasn't sure how all that had happened since Walt was only sixteen years old.

"I guess with the war, exceptions are made, "she stated

rather matter-of-factly as if that explained everything. Although she wasn't sure where Doug was stationed, she knew Johnny was in Bermuda. We laughed and talked the afternoon away as if we had never been apart. Walter picked us up on his way home from work.

Riding the bus to Northridge the next day, we visited Madeline with Mom. We had always received more letters from her than anyone, so we knew she had kids, Freddie, Joyce, Bobby, and Dreama. I hadn't seen Freddie since he was that tiny, little boy in the shoebox. It was a thrill to see how strong and healthy he was now. Just as it had been with Franie, we were as comfortable with Madeline as if we had seen her every day. We talked, laughed and played with her kids all afternoon. We rode the bus back to Mom's, where she fixed supper while Lee and I listened to the radio and relaxed out on the front stoop.

On Tuesday, Mom decided we would just stay around the house for the day. Walter went off to work and we went outside to scout out the neighborhood. Dayton was a lot bigger than Grundy, but Mom didn't have any inclination to take us anywhere or do anything special with us. She let us wander around knowing we would find our way back. That evening, she and Walter played gin rummy with us. It was fun and we laughed and talked as we figured families did regularly. Not having any experience at being family, Lee and I were just guessing. Before going to bed that night, she assured us that we would go see Loretta the next day.

It was late afternoon when we left for Loretta's. She had a job at Seville restaurant and wouldn't be home until after 3:00, according to Mom. Her apartment was on Brown Street, the complete opposite end of town from where Franie and Madeline lived. She had always been more independent and adventurous than her sisters and we were looking forward to seeing her. Even though she had never written at the school, we were sure she would want to see us, now that we were here in town. We were looking forward to whatever stories she had to tell us and we were sure she had some. Not having seen her since she had left the shanty boat, we were more curious about her than we had been about Franie or Madeline. I wasn't even sure she would recognize us, as we were little boys when she had last seen us and now we were both young men. Not too surprising, she was a little standoffish when she first opened the door, but after crushing hugs from Lee and I, she warmed considerably. She made no excuse for not writing, but began telling us all that had happened to her since we had last seen her.

"Madeline wrote and told us you were married and then divorced," I told her, "and that you were living in Charleston. That was about all we knew." I stated.

"Well, she was right. I stayed there a couple years and then went to Huntington," she explained. "I knew Franie was there and I got a job as a nursemaid."

"When did you come here?" Lee asked her.

"Well, I guess it was shortly after Franie had moved here." she began, "I had been to Dayton before to visit Aunt Dottie, but didn't stay then because she had too many rules and she wouldn't let me smoke." She continued telling us about her different jobs and different homes and then surprised us with an unexpected twist. "I joined the WACS in 1942, shortly after Pearl Harbor," she announced. "I thought I could help the boys who had joined." She explained that she had been sent to Knoxville, Tennessee for basic training and then on to Bangor, Maine to a duty station. She was twenty-one years old at the time. "When the government decided to make the WACS a part of the regular Army I had been in for six months," she continued with her story, "They offered us a release if we didn't want to stay. The WACS had turned out to not be what I thought they were so I took their offer." She paused while she lit a cigarette, "I went down to Yonkers, New York and got a job. I only stayed three months before I decided to come on back here where my sisters were living." she finished her tale. We gazed at her with newfound respect. She was quite a woman of the world to us, like some of them in the movies we had seen. Asking about us, we briefly told her about the school, our jobs, friends and Pop Hurley. "You boys look like you're doing ok," she said. "You've sure grown since I saw you last." We knew that was certainly true. It was almost suppertime and Mom was anxious to get home before Walter, so we hurriedly said our goodbyes and left. We knew we probably wouldn't see Loretta again for quite some time, but we were pretty use to goodbyes by now.

Our last couple of days in Dayton was a flurry of visits from Madeline and Franie. Wanting to see as much of us as they could, they had come to Mom's, not waiting for her to take us to them. Waking us early on Saturday morning, we were in the car before the sun came up. Mom had packed peanut butter sandwiches for us as we headed back to Virginia. We stopped along the side of the road to stretch our legs and eat our lunch. Walter had bought us a RC cola to drink with our sandwiches when he had stopped for gas. Climbing back into the Chevy, we settled down for the final ride back to the school. We arrived before supper and with a brief goodbye, they were gone. Only God knew when and if we would ever see Mom again. She had given us no reason to expect anything more from her than the rare visit.

Meeting Don, Mose and E.C. for supper felt good. I was home again, where things were comfortable and familiar for me. I was sure Lee felt the same way, as he had found his buddies quickly, too. Don and E.C. had been gone at the same time we were, Mose told me. They both still had Dads and had gone to spend a week with them.

"Good to have you all back," he said. "Been pretty strange around here without you." We quickly fell back into our normal joking, laughing, talking, and eyeballing the girls. Although I had enjoyed seeing my sisters and catching up on my brothers, it was good to be back among friends and where we felt comfortable.

Mose, E.C., Don, and I had discovered a gem up on the side of the lush, green mountain that stood directly behind our school. Although difficult to reach, as it was underneath a cliff overhang, it was well worth the effort. We had to crawl on our bellies, along the side of the mountain, make our way underneath the overhang, before finally reaching a good-sized cave in the mountainside. It would make a great hideout for a group of orphan boys, we decided, when we first made our discovery. Knowing that none of the adults from Mountain Mission School, where we lived, would make the climb up, we knew it was perfect. We spent many a Saturday and Sunday afternoon in our favorite spot, inviting other friends as we chose.

Aware that E.C., Mose and a few other friends had gone on ahead; I decided I was tired of eating the same thing everyday. Although I was thankful for any food, pinto beans, potatoes and cornbread had gotten old after four years. I wanted something different and had dreams about Aunt Nora's cooking. I knew what I had in mind, as I had been planning it for some weeks now. Strolling, nonchalantly around the chicken coops, I made sure no one was around. Quickly, I reached down and snatching one of the chickens, I high tailed it for the cave. Being only fourteen, I climbed the mountain with no problem and approached the cave opening. The boys had heard me coming and were waiting at the opening to see what I was carrying.

"How about some chicken for supper," I exclaimed.

"Where'd you get that?" E.C. questioned, already knowing the answer.

"Stole it, "I offered. "You want some?" I asked, as the boys gathered around. "I'll wring its neck myself," I told them, "I remember seeing my Aunt Nora do it." I explained, feeling pretty cocky and sure of myself. "If you guys help me pluck the feathers, I'll do the rest,"I concluded.

"If we're all eating, then we're all helping, "Mose answered. All of us had seen women boil water to dunk the chicken into before plucking it, but we didn't have any water in the cave. Going for some would take too long and would be difficult to haul up the mountain we decided. Instead, we would just pluck it dry. Mose began building a fire to roast it on, while we started pulling feathers out like a bunch of lunatics. We let them flutter down the mountain as we tossed them outside the cave. Just as we stood back to check out our handiwork, the chicken jumped up. Shaking its head, as if a little dazed, she took off, heading for the light at the cave opening. Momentarily stunned, we froze in place.

"I thought it was dead," Tommy yelled, as we all came to our senses.

"I must have just put it to sleep, " I responded in shock. We ran to catch it before it reached the cliff and got away. Just as I got to it, the chicken jumped off the cliff, flapping its featherless wings, trying to fly. The poor chicken flapped and flapped, unable to get any air under its naked wings. It began tumbling, falling and running naked down the mountainside. We were right behind it, laughing so hard at how pathetic it looked we could hardly run. In spite of our laughter, we were still determined to catch it for supper and ran as fast as we could down the mountain.

As we neared the bottom, E.C. stopped suddenly and reminded us, "If Pop Hurley catches us with that chicken down here, he'll skin us alive." Knowing this was true; we decided we'd rather give up the chicken than to incur Pop's wrath for stealing. We returned to the school from the other side to avoid him.

Pop had just returned from the dairy farm when the chicken ran passed him. Startled, he glanced around for some of the kids. Spotting me from a ways off, he hollered for me to come to him.

"Paul, get over here, "he commanded, waving me to him. "We've got a problem with one of the chickens," he explained when I reached him. "One of them just ran pass me, with not a single feather on its body. I'm not sure what's wrong with it, but it must have some kind of disease," he continued. "We can't have the rest of the chickens getting sick and dying. You go find it, kill it and bury it on the far end of the field."

Not knowing if he knew the truth or truly believed the chicken was sick, I didn't hesitate, "Yes, sir. I'll take care of it right away," I answered, as I rushed to the chicken coop, knowing better than to disobey Pop. Wondering if I was going to be able to sneak the bird back to the cave after all, I quickly had my answer. Catching the naked chicken, I glanced around to see Pop still standing where I had left him, watching all that I was doing. In that brief moment, I knew he suspected something, but couldn't put his finger on it. He wouldn't act on suspicion, that much I knew. I had learned my lesson, however, and knew the Good Lord had given me a reprieve from stealing. I was never going to be eating chicken in our cave, unless I bought and paid for it. That was completely clear to me.

Before long, the summer was gone; school had started again and with it, all the preparations necessary for winter. As Don and I walked back from the cornfields, we grabbed a handful of apples from Mr. White's tree. They were hanging over the fence, just asking to be picked. We didn't really think of it as stealing, even though, I guess it was, since we hadn't asked him for them. Taking a few more than we wanted for ourselves, we had a plan in mind for the others. We went inside the dorm, cleaned up and headed for supper. We had stashed our apples until we had finished supper, knowing it wouldn't be dark yet and we could carry out our plan.

Rows of trees separated the girl's dorm from ours. As we had gotten older, we had discovered the girls taking occasional strolls after supper on their side of the trees. Deciding amongst ourselves that perhaps they were as interested in us, as we were in them, we took the strolls as an invitation. Using the apples as an excuse to talk to them, Don had taken some over and had given them to one of the girls. SMACK right across my face came Pop's enormous hand! He had never slapped me in the face and so shocked by what had happened, I cried out as he accused me of giving apples to the girls.

"It wasn't me, Pop," I yelled. My face was on fire and I fought to control myself. Fortunately for me, as I was about to do something stupid, Pop glanced around and immediately realized his mistake.

"There he is, that's the one I saw," he stated as he took off after Don, without a word of apology to me. Although I knew I had gotten away with things in the past and not been punished, I was terribly hurt by Pop's slap in the face for something I had not done. I never forgot his lack of an apology, either.

My birthday passed once again without any notice. There were no cards from my Mom or sisters and no mention of it by anyone at the school. In fact, letters from home had become almost non-existent since Lee and I's visit. Nothing much changed at the school, year to year. I still had my chores, the routine of each day remained the same and my friends and I continued to hang out together. Thanksgiving and Christmas continued to be a highlight of our year. I couldn't believe it was 1944 already. Fifteen years old, I was beginning to think about life down the road and what may be in store for me. With all I had to do though, I didn't have much time to ponder about it and those thoughts came rarely.

Winter dragged on, and Pop, not being a complete fuddy-duddy, decided that we needed something to break up the boredom. He was not totally unaware that young men and young women craved each other's attention. Needing to control that situation, something that I wouldn't completely understand until I was a parent myself, he announced after chapel that we would have a box lunch auction that Saturday evening. For those who had never experienced this, he explained that the girls would make up a meal in a box and the boys would be allowed to bid on whichever girl's meal they wanted. Whoever won the bid would then, not only win the meal, but also the privilege of eating the meal with the young lady. The place erupted with applause as Pop excused us and sent us on our way. The girls appeared as delighted as we boys were at this wonderful turn of events. We rushed to school, intent on dropping hints to the girl of our choice.

None of us thought Saturday evening would ever arrive. E.C., Don, Mose, and I had picked out the girl of our choice and made sure we had as much money as we could muster. We all gathered in the auditorium waiting impatiently for the bidding to start. The girls marched in with their boxes and placed them on a long table. Miss Spring and Mom Hurley gave them a number to hold and placed the matching number on their box. Everyone was present, from the smallest to the oldest. Pop had included everyone, even though he knew the teenagers would be the ones winning the bids. Of course, some of the girls had brothers at the school that made sure the price was raised for any boy who wanted their sister's box lunch. None of us cared though, as this was the first opportunity we had to have a kind of a date with a girl and we knew the money was for the school anyway. Pop began the bidding. Mose won his bid first and beaming went to gather his meal and his girl. Although they were allowed to take a seat together, no one could eat until all the boxes were gone.

"Number 23," Pop hollered out Arizona's number.

I almost choked as I called out my bid, "$1.00." $1.25, the bid went up.

"$1.50," I countered. $1.75 came another bid and then $2.00 from someone else.

" $2.25," I responded. I was not going to give up as I had money from my paper route and I really wanted to eat with the tall, blond Arizona. $2.50 was the quick response.

"$2.75," I countered again. Waiting, Pop held his gavel. Nothing.

"Going once." Nothing. " Going twice." Nothing. " Sold to you, Paul," he announced. Finally taking a breath, I rushed forward to claim my meal and my girl. She was mine at least for that evening. E.C. and Don had also won their bids for the girls they wanted and we all gathered at one table.

Everyone was a little shy and unsure of themselves as we began opening up the boxes and sharing the meal. We soon relaxed and began enjoying the evening together, eating, talking and flirting. Suddenly, without any warning, the auditorium went black. Every light in the place had gone out and a number of the girls let out a yell. Pop's voice came from the blackness, attempting to calm everyone.

"Please, don't anyone move from your seat. I don't want anyone hurt. Dean and I will see what is going on. Stay calm." I couldn't have been more pleased, as Arizona had grabbed onto me out of fear, I guess. How lucky can I get, I thought. Taking advantage of the total blackness, I stole a few hugs and kisses before Pop returned. "The entire school is out of lights," he explained. "Dean and Mr. Taylor have gone into town to see what has happened. The entire town looks dark though." It had become apparent to me that Arizona was enjoying the darkness and my closeness as much as I was hers. Knowing that the darkness hid us from everyone, with the possible exception of our table, we continued holding each other and necking discreetly. I was sure my buddies were taking advantage of the dark, also. The lights could stay out as far as I was concerned.

Much too soon for me, Dean Sublett returned with the news that there was a huge fire in town at the power station and much of Grundy was in danger. Everyone was without power and they were still fighting the fire. Mr. Taylor had stayed in town to help. As much as we were enjoying the girls, this definitely got our attention.

"Do we need to go help?" One of the older boys' voices rang out.

"We can if they need us," someone else added. Pop immediately took charge and told us we would be needed here to help get the smaller children back to the dorms safely.

"There are enough men in town to take care of their situation," he stated. "I think we better just take care of things here." Asking everyone to stay seated, he and Dean left to fetch some kerosene lamps that they had for emergencies.

Returning with the lamps, he lit one and handed it to Mom

and another to Miss Springer and Miss Young. Instructing the girls to line up behind one of the ladies, he knew the older ones would see that the younger ones were taken care of. The auditorium was in the same building as the girl's rooms and the lamps provided enough light for them to get safely down the hall and to their rooms. I hated to let Arizona go, but the mood had been broken already by the commotion. Pop knew that once we got outside, we would have some starlight to see by, but he didn't want any of the smaller boys to be left behind. Dean Sublett, Aunt Sis and Pop managed to gather the boys outside the dorm, and asking us to wait there, he returned to the auditorium to check for anyone who may not have gotten outside yet.

"Each of you older boys, get a hold of a smaller one with each hand," Pop asked. "We'll all walk together." It was pitch black outside even with the stars. With no lights from anywhere in the school and none from town, it was really strange. We all managed to get to the dorm, and after escorting the smaller boys to their beds, we found our way to ours with no problem.

"Wow, that was some night, wasn't it?" I commented to E.C.

"Sure was a good one," he answered me as we pulled the blanket over us. I was sure he wasn't talking about the lights either.

By morning, the lights were back on at the school. We didn't need them though, as the glow from that evening wasn't going to leave us boys for a while, I was sure, and the girls seemed much more relaxed as well. I guess quite a bit of sexual tension had been released that evening. Unfortunately, Grundy had suffered some damage to the town, but Pop made us available to do all we could to help. No one minded, as we knew they would have done the same for us had the shoe been on the other foot.

"When I grow up and get out of here, I'm never hoeing another row of corn in my life," Lee complained as we worked planting the fields that spring. Planting corn on a hillside is hard work. Not being able to use any equipment, the ground has to be turned over by hand. If you don't stay above the boys turning the ground over, they cover your rows with their dirt. Every seed has to be planted by hand and even young backs get sore by the end of planting time. Lee worked as hard as anyone and never shirked his duties, but he hated it. I'm sure he won't be a farmer when he grows up, I chuckled to myself. He was thirteen now, but to me he was still that little, red-haired, freckled faced kid I needed to take care of. Maybe he always would be to me, but I didn't mind.

Before long, all the planting was done and the furnace had been shut down for the year. My paper route continued to keep me busy along with my other chores. Summer meant extra time with my buddies and our obsession with the girls. I seemed to get paddled every time I turned around that summer of 1944, either for trying to sneak and see a girl or for smoking. I couldn't seem to leave either one alone. I wasn't the only one, though, as my buddies got almost as many as I did. At least over girls since none of them smoked. Finally, whether because he sympathized with us and our need for the girls company or simply to provide some different activity, Pop suggested we have a pie supper.

Similar to a box lunch auction, the girls each bake a pie and the boys bid on it for the honor of having dinner and pie with the girl who baked it. We were even more excited as it was summer and we seldom got to see the girls with school being out. Again scheduled for Saturday night, I knew exactly whose pie I wanted. Lena was a short, dark-haired, well-built young lady I had been eyeing for quite some time. I knew I wouldn't care what kind she baked, I was going to win her pie for the evening. "Do we want to go to the movies today?" Mose asked Don and I.

"How much money do you have?" I asked. "We want to make sure we have enough for tonight."

"I think I'm ok. You ok, Mose?" Don asked. Mose nodded yes.

"The day will take forever to pass if we don't do something," I stated, "but we don't want to come up short either. I've got my paper money, so I'm ok if you guys are." The three of us finally agreed to head to the movies. E.C. had gone to visit his Dad and we knew he would be disappointed to miss the pie supper. The war was still going on and we watched the newsreel hoping for an end soon. I hadn't heard from anyone, so I figured no news was good news when it came to my brothers. Surely, someone would have written if something had happened to them, I supposed. We left the movies and instantly began talking about the girls we hoped to be eating pie with that night. "Don't suppose we'd be lucky enough to have another lights out, do you?" Mose stated. Laughing we made our way back to the dorm in anticipation of the evenings delights.

As had been the case before, the girls had been given numbers for them and for their pies. The entire room smelled delicious with the various pies having just been baked that day. My friends and I could hardly contain ourselves as we waited for Pop to begin the bidding. Ten or twelve pies had been sold when Don won his bid. Escorting his girl to the table, they watched as the bidding resumed. Pop reached for Lena's pie and I was ready.

"$1.00," I offered knowing I would not get it for that. $1.50 came a bid.

"$2.00," I answered. $2.25 came another offer from a voice

I knew I recognized. Turning to see where it came from, I saw Dean Sublett bidding against me.

"$2.50," I answered stubbornly and just as stubbornly he responded, "$2.75."

"$3.00," I said glancing his way.

"$3.25," he answered, as he grinned at me. I suddenly realized, he wasn't interested in Lena or the pie. He simply wanted to see how bad I wanted it and to make sure she got a fair price.

"$3.50," I stated. No response. Pop seemed to be in on the plan and hesitated, glancing at Dean.

Shaking his head no, Pop finished, "Going once, going twice, sold to Paul." I walked forward to get Lena and her pie and Pop smiled a sneaky little smile at me. They had enjoyed the bidding I was sure and it had all been in good fun. The auction continued with Mose getting the girl he wanted and joining our table. We waited patiently, enjoying sitting close to our chosen girls and watching the activity.

Eating our supper and pie together was about the most enjoyable evening I had ever had at the school. Maybe the box lunch affair had made me a little more comfortable with a girl, I don't know. I just know that this evening was relaxing and enjoyable from start to finish. Oh, no, we weren't lucky enough to have the lights go out again, but I know I was able to steal one kiss anyway and I imagine Don and Mose did too. We escorted the girls to the exit of the auditorium, since Pop wouldn't allow us any further, and said our goodnights. Dean Sublett caught up with me as I was leaving,

"Well, I guess you really wanted that pie?" he asked me laughing.

"You sure made me pay for it didn't you, sir." I told him.

"Well, I hoped you knew I was just playing with you. Wanted to help the girl out," he explained.

"Well I was surprised at first, but then I knew you were teasing me."

Pop showed up then and asked, "You ok, boy?" I figured he had been in on the joke with Dean.

"Yea, I'm ok, "I answered him. "I didn't really mind. She was worth every penny." We reached the dorm and said our goodnights. Having the bed to myself, as E.C. was still away, I just laid there thinking about Lena long into the night.

Dean and Mrs. Sublett

E.C. had returned in time for lunch on Sunday and we all decided to go to the river for a swim, as it was a hot, still, August afternoon. The water coming out of the mountains was always cool, if not cold, and diving in sent delightful shocks all over our bodies. The river was deep and wide at our special spot and a huge willow tree stood almost in the water with its branches hanging out over it. We had a great time climbing the tree and diving into the water, knowing it was plenty deep. There were two thick grapevines to swing from as well and we climbed, swung, dived, and swam the entire afternoon away, knowing that summer would soon end. Sunday afternoons were the best. No work, no school, nothing but relaxing and sharing time with friends.

The summer was ending when a package and letter arrived from my sister, Franie. I had never received any package from anyone and I was anxious to see what was inside. Without reading the letter, I ripped open the box to find a nice, slightly worn, sport coat that appeared to be my size or at least close to it. Not sure why she would have sent it to me, I opened her letter, curious as to how she had come by it. I was shocked to read that her husband, Jim, had died of tuberculosis recently and she wanted me to have his coat. I had no idea he had been ill, as no one had written to let us know. I wrote her to let her know I was sorry and to thank her, but I didn't know any more to do. I hoped Madeline and Loretta could help her since they were there with her.

I was in the tenth grade when school resumed and would soon turn sixteen. Mose was in twelfth grade and would be graduating at the end of the year. He had not said what his plans were and none of us wanted to ask. E.C. and Don were a year ahead of me, but never made anything of it. Not attending school wasn't an option, but for whatever reason I had never learned to care much for it. Even though I loved and respected Miss Spring, my favorite teacher, I never grasped the importance of school, I guess. I knew Pop had never finished school and he had become very successful in my eyes. Maybe his lack of education bothered him and was why he insisted on it for us. I just knew it was something I had to do and accepted it. Besides, my friends were there and we were pretty much inseparable.

School Buddies on a Saturday Afternoon
Mose standing in middle, Paul on right, E.C. lower left

Firing the furnace remained my job and as the cooler weather returned, so did my birthday. I had discovered a hidden benefit in my job that had previously went unnoticed by me. Perhaps, my growing interest in girls had gotten my attention, but not many adults were stirring when I left the dorm to tend to the furnace in the mornings. The girls, however, had to be at the kitchen by five o'clock in the morning to begin preparations for breakfast. By secretly passing Arizona, the girl who I was with when the lights had gone out earlier in the year, a note at school, I was able to arrange a meeting outside the dining hall. Making sure I had shaved and applied my Mennen's After Shave to be as enticing and desirable as I knew how, I showed up hoping she would accept my invitation. I was extremely pleased when I saw the door open and Arizona peek out. I motioned her outside and convincing her we were safely hidden, engaged in some serious hugging and kissing. That was all we dared risk, but to us it was daring and exciting. I was sure she was the girl for me forever. I was always concerned that we would be caught and, although, I didn't care for myself, I had been paddled plenty already, I did care for her. Surprisingly, she was the only girl Pop never caught me with and we continued meeting on a regular basis.

It wasn't long before Thanksgiving had arrived. It didn't matter how many Thanksgivings I had been here for, every one was special and I looked forward to the day. Everything about it I enjoyed, from the special chapel service to the sandwiches for supper and everything in between. It was good to know that this day would always be celebrated exactly as it had been before and that Christmas would be, too. Sure enough, a couple weeks after Thanksgiving, we began getting ready for Christmas and all the celebration that went with it. It was a grand time for all of us.

Christmas arrived and being older now, I enjoyed the

excitement of the smaller children as much as I enjoyed the day myself. For a lot of them, just as it had been for me, this was their first real Christmas and the delight in their eyes warmed you inside. There were always children being added to the school, it seemed. As the older ones left, new ones arrived. Sometimes entire families, sometimes one child at a time. That Christmas, I remembered how good I had felt to know I was, finally, safe, warm, and fed and I hoped they felt the same way. Lee had never acted in the Christmas play, as he had decided he would rather watch, than act. As the Christmas play began, I could see him with his eyes glued to the stage, totally enthralled with it all. The day was a total success as far as I was concerned. The church service, the meal, the brown paper bag, the gifts, and dessert, nothing had been left out and I went to bed that night perfectly content.

January 1945 arrived with the coldest weather of the year. I was spending quite a few nights in the furnace room to keep the fire going. I had been doing it so long, I never gave it a second thought. Arizona and I continued to have our morning rendezvous' as often as we could, ignoring the cold for the few stolen minutes of intimacy. We were having a good time getting away with something for a change, almost as much as we were enjoying each other. I was kept pretty busy though, with the furnace, my paper route, school and trying to sneak a few minutes with her as often as I could. I looked forward to the weather improving and the furnace job easing up some.

Sometimes, bad winters turn around and give you delightful springs. That was the case this spring of 1945. By the end of March, the days were mostly all warm and Pop allowed me to bank the furnace daily. It was Sunday morning when I made a decision that would change everything for me. I had fired up the furnace to take the morning chill off the buildings, delivered my papers, and met my buddies for breakfast. We talked and laughed as we ate and headed to church together. I had a plan in my head, but I didn't want to tell anyone just yet. Sitting quietly through our church service, my idea grew and grew in my head. Deciding to keep quiet for a while longer, we left church and walked over to the dining hall for lunch.

"Want to go up to the cave this afternoon?" E.C. asked me.

"Maybe, later," I told him, "I'll have to bank the furnace and I need to talk to Lee first." Not thinking anything about that, he agreed.

"Well, give a holler when you're done," he said, "I'll be around somewhere."

I decided to find Lee and explain what I had in mind before I banked the furnace.

"Hey, brother," I called to him as he was heading to his room. Stopping, he let me catch up to him. As we got to his room, I checked to be sure his roommate wasn't inside and quietly said, "I'm going to leave the school for good today. I'm going to Dayton."

His eyes almost popped out of his head and he immediately said, "Well, I'm going with you." Wishing I didn't have to say what I was about to, I took a deep breath and told him what I had already decided.

"No, you stay here. I don't know how I'm getting there or how hard it may be, but I promise you, if you'll stay here, I'll have you out and with me in no more than thirty days. O.K?" Without much argument, he agreed.

"I'd rather go now," he said.

"I know, but its better this way. I won't leave you here. You know that." I consoled him. That part having been taken care of, I then asked, "Do you have any money?"

"A little I think," he answered fishing in his pockets, "You can have it all." He handed me every dime he had, a total of $1.30.

"That'll help," I told him. "I've got a couple bucks. Should get me a ways down the road."

Staring at me, he finally asked, "When you leaving?"

"Just as soon as I bank the furnace," I answered. "No one will look for me on a Sunday afternoon and I'll be long gone by supper time." Not very good at goodbyes, I quickly left calling over my shoulder, "See you soon, brother." As I passed my room, I grabbed the Bible Miss Spring had given me and sticking my toothbrush in my pocket, went to bank the furnace for the last time.

I made sure I did an excellent job that last time as I knew Pop would be furious I had ran away, but I didn't want him to think I had ever done a poor job. Looking around as I exited the furnace room, I made sure none of my buddies was around. I would have liked to have told them I was leaving, but I felt safer doing it this way. No one had any idea, except Lee, and I knew he would never tell anyone. I hadn't really planned on running away. Nothing had happened that had made me angry or upset. I had been given a good life at the school and, truth be told, they had probably saved my life, I knew. Only God knew where I might have ended up had it not been for Pop Hurley. I simply woke up this morning and knew I was leaving.

Strolling nonchalantly down the road that led to town, I was sure no one would pay me any mind this afternoon. Having been to church that morning, I was still dressed in my Sunday best, a pair of good pants, dress shirt and the sport coat Franie had sent me. At sixteen, I was allowed to go wherever I wanted, except to the girl's dorm, on a Sunday and I hadn't changed clothes, figuring nice clothes might get me a ride easier when I ran out of money. I continued down the main road leading out of town. Waiting until I was well out of sight of anyone at the school or town, I flagged down the bus as it approached.

"How far can I get on this?" I asked the bus driver when he opened his door.

"Well, you ain't got much. What is that, not even $2.00?" he examined the money in my hand. "I can take you just into West Virginia, if that's the direction you're going," he offered.

Jumping onto the bus, I answered him, "That'd be just fine." Settling down for the ride, I finally relaxed a little. Knowing I still had a long way to go, at least I was out of Pop's reach now.

It didn't seem to take no time and the bus arrived at a small town just over the West Virginia line. I had noticed the name but quickly forgotten it, figuring it didn't matter anyhow. I was headed to Logan and hoped to catch a ride. I hadn't walked but a mile or so, when an older man in a pick-up truck stopped and offered me a ride. The good Lord was sure on my side, I thought to myself.

"Where you going, boy?" he asked.

"Going to Ohio," I said, quickly adding when I noticed his surprised look at me, "But hope to get to Logan before dark. Got some friends there."

"Passing right through there," he said.

"Much obliged," I answered as he motioned for me to get in the truck. He was a friendly sort and I enjoyed the ride, as he did most of the talking.

"Just where in Logan you want to go," he asked as we neared town.

"I'm going to just the other side," I explained, "but I can get out wherever you want."

"No, no," he said, "I'm going on past Logan, so just give a yell when you want out." We drove on through Logan and about two miles down the road, I spotted Qinny and Hotdog's place.

"This is good, right here," I said. Thanking him and apologizing for not having any money, he shooed me away.

"No need," he said, "I was coming this way anyway and enjoyed the company. You take care now," he advised me as he drove off.

I hadn't seen Quinny or Hotdog for years and I tentatively approached their door. They had been friends of Moms for years and, although they knew me when I was much smaller, I wasn't sure they'd know me after this long. It was certainly a relief when Quinny grabbed me and dragged me into her house having recognized me immediately. What a relief I said to myself, since I sure wasn't looking forward to having to sleep out in the cold and dark if she hadn't.

"What you doing in our neck of the woods?" she asked as she set me down at the table.

"I ran away from Mount Mission School." I told her, knowing she would understand.

"Your Mom had told me you were there," she said. "Where's Lee? Wasn't he with you?" I explained that I thought it best to leave by myself and then send for him when I had bus money for him.

"Could I stay here a few days?" I asked her; pretty sure, she would agree. Quinny was a good person and would help anyone who needed her. "I need to get a job so I can get bus fare to Dayton," I continued.

"Stay as long as you like," she answered as I knew she would, "Might get a job over at the Sugar Bowl in Logan," she added. She had been fixing supper when I arrived and continued as she talked to me. About then, Hotdog came in and saw me.

"Well, look what the cat drug in," he said. "Good to see you, boy. Been a while." Hotdog was a skinny, rugged coal miner and as we ate supper I told him, what I had been doing and what my plan was now. "We'll help all we can," he offered as we finished our supper.

Although Hotdog worked at the coalmine directly across the river, they chose to live on this side of the river instead of in the coal camp that was over there. A decent, three bedroom house, it was a bit nicer than the coal camp houses. Maryanne and Sara were their two daughters and you couldn't ask for more pleasant girls. Barely older than me, I didn't see them as possible dates as I did most available girls, but instead as sisters to me. I'm sure they felt the same way. Agreeing to double up, Sara gave me her bed for as long as I needed it she said. I was relieved when I slipped into bed that night knowing that I was welcome here.

I woke up to the sounds and smells of the family stirring. I quickly got out of bed, dressed and went to the kitchen to see if there was anything, I could do to help. Quinny was fixing breakfast and after asking how I slept, told me to sit down for breakfast. Before I could object, Hotdog and the girls arrived, as if on cue.

When Quinny placed eggs on my plate, I told her, "This is the first eggs I've had since last Easter."

Giving me a quizzical look, she asked, "Easter?"

"Yes, it's the only time we got them," I said, "too many of us for every day."

"Well, be sure you enjoy them then," she said, "and have some potatoes and biscuits, too." I ate my fill and explained that I needed to go into Logan to see about a job if Quinny didn't need me to do anything for her.

"Going to check at the Sugar Bowl like you said," I told her as I prepared to leave. "If I'm not back by supper, you'll know I'm working and I'll be here when I'm done. Is that ok?" I asked her.

"Sure, son, you do what you got to do. Get back when you can." Quinny assured me. Hotdog had already taken his rowboat and rowed across the river to the mine and the girls were preparing for school when I walked out, hoping to catch a ride into Logan.

I got lucky that morning, as there were men on their way to work in Logan and I quickly hitched a ride with one of them. The Sugar Bowl was on this side of town and I asked to be let out as we approached. I wasn't shy about asking for work and the manager seemed to admire my gumption.

"Need a dishwasher and busboy," he offered, "for lunch and supper. Interested?" Willing to do whatever he needed, I quickly accepted.

"Yes sir, I sure am."

"Pays fifty cents a day and I'll pay you at the end of the week," he advised me.

"Can I start today?" I asked him.

"Can start right now if you want. Lunch crowd will be coming in before long.," he said. Showing me what he wanted me to do; I quickly caught on and was ready when the first customers arrived. He had a pretty fair business for lunch, but supper was even busier. Finally washing my last dish, I made sure everything was in order and asked if I could leave.

"See you tomorrow?" he said with a question in his voice.

"Yes sir," I told him, "Be here bright and early."

"Don't have to be too early," he said, "I don't have much breakfast crowd. Ten o'clock will be fine." I hurried outside hoping to catch a ride back to Quinny and Hotdogs. It was dusk dark and I didn't see a car on the road, so I walked the two miles back to the house.

It was about eight o'clock by the time I arrived and Quinny was waiting to hear my news.

"Must of got a job," she stated as I arrived at the door.

"Yep, just like you said. Dishwasher at the Sugar Bowl," I told her.

"Go put these on," she told me, handing me a pair of Hotdog's bib overalls. "Bring me those clothes you have on. I need to wash them for you for tomorrow," she instructed me.

"You don't have to do that," I said, "I can do it."

Giving me a stern look, she stated, "Just do what I told you. Then get over here and eat your supper." Knowing to do what she said, I slipped into the bedroom and changed, bringing her my dirty clothes. Sitting down at the table, she handed me a plate of food she had saved from their supper. I realized how hungry I was at that point and told her so. Quinny was a short, plump, happy woman who seemed to enjoy taking care of her family and now me, too. She quickly had my clothes washed and hanging to dry before I had finished eating.

By the time I woke up for breakfast the next morning, she had ironed my clothes and laid them on a chair in my room. I couldn't believe anyone would be so kind to me, but she was. She followed the same routine every day as, she fed me breakfast, sent me off to the Sugar Bowl, took my clothes when I came home, fed me supper, and washed and ironed my clothes everyday.

When I told her how much I appreciated it, she simply said, "Can't let you go out of here dirty, now, can I?" She thought nothing of it and I don't think I could have stopped her if I had tried. I was a little disappointed when the week was over. I knew I would be leaving as soon as I got my pay and I didn't know if I would ever see her, Hotdog, or the girls again.

Monday morning I said my goodbyes after breakfast and thanking all of them for their hospitality, I quickly left. I caught a ride into Logan and stopping at the Sugar Bowl, I told the manager that I was quitting my job. After explaining to him that I was going to Ohio where my family was, he understood and gave me my $3.50 pay.

"Good luck, boy," he called after me as I headed for the bus station. Approaching the ticket station, I asked if $4.00 would get me to Dayton, Ohio. I had a little money left from when I had left the school. Assuring me that I had enough, the man gave me my ticket and pointed me to my bus. Finding a window seat, I was relieved to be on my way. My promise to Lee loomed in my head and I was determined to not let him down. First, I had to get to Dayton myself.

The bus rambled on and on and I slept some and watched the passing scenery some. Noticing the land getting flatter, I knew we must be getting close. I had been doing for myself for so long, I hadn't even thought of writing anyone to let them know I was coming. But then, I didn't know I was until that Sunday morning a week or so ago. Oh well, I thought, I'll find somewhere to sleep if I can't find one of my sisters. I wasn't worried about it and knew I could take care of myself. I hadn't even thought of trying to find Mom. The bus pulled into the Dayton bus station and I stepped out. Well, you're here, I thought. Now what!

I walked over to a bus driver who was taking a smoke and joined him. Pulling Madeline's last letter out of my pocket, I asked if he could give me directions.

"That's a pretty fair walk from here," he said, "Got any money? You need to catch a bus."

"I've got about 30 cents is all," I told him.

"Only takes a dime," he answered as he pointed me to the correct bus. "You can finish smoking," he said, "It won't take off just yet." Keeping an eye on the bus I needed to catch, I finished smoking and boarded the bus. A short ride and I was in front of Madeline's house. Not even sure if she still lived there, I knocked on the door and was pleased to hear her voice as she came to answer my knock.

"Oh, my God," she screamed, "How did you get here?"

Giving her a big hug, I told her," I ran away."

"Where's Lee?" she asked, knowing I always took care of him. I explained my plan to her and she agreed I had probably done the right thing.

"Can I stay with you for awhile?" I asked her. "I'll get a job tomorrow and help out if I can." I knew with the war still going on that jobs were plentiful and I had no intention of going back to school. I wasn't concerned about finding one.

"You know you can," she said as she smacked me gently on the arm. "I wouldn't have it any other way." I collapsed on the sofa and we talked and talked, catching up on everyone and everything. I felt so comfortable with her and it was, as before, like I had never been gone. We just seemed to have a connection to each other that was hard to explain. It was good to be with family and even though I had only had brief snatches of family life up to now, as I lay in bed that night, I knew this was right. I would never deny that Mount Mission School had been good to me. They had no doubt saved my life or at least had saved me from a life of want and despair. They had provided food, shelter and clothing to me for a number of years. Even more so, they had taught me responsibility, discipline, strong moral values, good work ethics, manners and the value of friends. I would always be grateful to them for that. Nevertheless, there is nothing quite like family and I was glad to finally be reunited with a part of my family, anyway.

I was up early the next morning and after breakfast, Madeline directed me to the Virginia Cafeteria.

"I'm sure you can get a job there washing dishes," she said, "at least until something better comes along." Giving me directions, she waited at the bus stop with me to make sure I caught the correct bus. A sign in the window at the cafeteria advertising for help made my search easy. They started me immediately washing dishes and busing tables. I didn't mind what the job was, as I simply wanted to get enough money to send for Lee and keep my word. Arriving back at Madeline's that evening I felt ten feet tall, knowing I had a job and some family to come home to at night.

Having come from a very structured environment where everyone respected each other and each person did their own chores, I was not prepared for laziness or bossiness. I was finishing my second week of work when a fellow busboy decided I was new and stupid and he could boss me around.

He yelled at me, "Boy, come here. Bus this table, " I balked.

"It's your table, bus it yourself, " I answered. I suppose he thought that by rushing over, getting in my face and glaring he was going to intimidate me. Well, he thought wrong and without thinking I punched him one time right in the face and he dropped to the floor.

"Can't have no fighting here you two, " the boss yelled as he rushed over having seen the confrontation. Reluctantly, he gave me my pay and fired me all the while telling me he hated to let me go. It was little consolation to me that he fired the other guy, also.

Heading home, I noticed a sign at White's Bakery for help. Applying for the job, I was hired and told I could start the next morning. I had no idea what I would be doing, but Madeline assured me that I could do whatever they asked. She seemed to understand why I had gotten fired and didn't make me feel bad.

"I would have done the same thing," she laughed. "You can't let people bully you around. Besides, the bakery job pays more anyway, doesn't it?"

"Yell, I think so," I told her, "I don't like being fired though, but maybe it was just as well."

Reporting to work at 6:00 a.m., I was put in the bread-making department. A step up from being a busboy, I thought. I wasn't making the bread itself, but taking it, forming it and putting it into loaf pans. Still, I enjoyed it. It was something completely different to me and more like a real job. There were plenty of opportunities to learn different skills and do different things if you were so inclined. I intended to keep this job and ignored anyone who seemed to be looking for trouble. With the money I was now making I knew I would be able to keep my word to Lee and get him home with me.

Two weeks later, I told Sis I had enough money and she agreed to send it in a letter to Lee. I was waiting at the bus station for him when he stepped off, not quite 30 days from when I had left him. I could tell he was glad I was there to meet him.

"I knew you'd be here," he said, "and I knew you would keep your word to me." Asking if Pop was upset with him leaving, he surprised me, "No, not since Sis had written a letter explaining, but he sure is mad at you for running away."

"I didn't know any other way to leave," I told him. I felt bad that I had disappointed Pop Hurley, but having Lee here and us being with family overshadowed my guilt. "C'mon, Madeline is waiting to see you," I told him, as we rushed over to catch the bus to Northridge. A new chapter was beginning in our lives together and I was anxious to get started.

Epilogue

Paul continued working at the bakery until November. Over the months he had reconnected with Franie, Loretta and his Mom. His brothers were all still serving in the Armed Forces. Having turned 17 years old in October, he got his mom to agree to sign for him to join the Navy. With the end of the war, he hoped that by joining he could allow someone who had served during the war to be released. After the Navy, he obtained a job at General Motors in Dayton and married Janie Weisgarber. Shortly after that, he was together with all of his brothers, sisters and Mother for the first time since his Dad had been killed. He spent a lot of time with his family, especially his four brothers, for the next couple years. When Doug died at only 26 from an injury that had occurred during the war, the family began to scatter, moving to various parts of the country to raise their own families.

Not being able to have children, probably due to mumps going down on him, Paul and Janie adopted a son, Brian, at the age of 3 months. Paul became a supervisor at GM even though he had never graduated high school and was named to the Factory Management Council two years in a row. Divorced after 25 years, he married Judy Helterbrand and adopted her son, David.

Paul always made sure that he never allowed anyone to feel sorry for him because of his childhood and many people tried. "You don't miss what you never had" he would tell them when they questioned him about his childhood and lack of parents. "I survived and have had a good life," he would continue. He never allowed his past to make him bitter or angry. He appreciated Mount Mission School and all they had meant to him. His religious training at the school helped him forgive his Mother as he matured.

He retired from GM after 34 years and continued working at various jobs he enjoyed for another 10 years. Married to Judy for 28 years, he is now 77 years old and the proud grandfather of six grandchildren. Two from Brian and Nancy and four from David and Missy. Although he has some health issues at this time, he is happy and feels good and is thankful to God for all his blessings.

Lee married and moved to Florida. He is the proud father of two daughters, a son and five grandchildren. Widowed, he has since married and currently lives in South Carolina. Healthy and content with life, he and Paul have always remained close.

Printed in the United States
63983LVS00002B/100-102

9 781424 142019